& CREATIVE STUDIES

TRIPLE TESTED • FOR YOUR SUCCESS EVERY TIME

As cooks you're nothing if not adventurous, and your acceptance of every kind of Asian noodle, as confirmed by a look in your pantry or at your suburb's local noodle bar, is nothing short of phenomenal. Because of their sheer number and ways to cook them, noodles present themselves as endless culinary possibilities — now seems a good time to introduce you to a whole new repertoire of recipes filled with *Oodles of Noodles*.

Pamela Clark

FOOD EDITOR

OODLES *of* NOODLES

Contents

⊏ **A picture is worth a thousand words...** Noodle packaging information can sometimes be misleading or even incorrectly translated so it's important that you can actually identify what's inside the package, regardless of what name the manufacturer has given it. To help, we've included a sample of each noodle, before it was cooked, in the same picture as the finished dish in which it's used.

Noodles, by any other name...

Don't worry if you can't find exactly the same noodle we call for: as long as you use one made from the same basic ingredient (wheat flour, rice flour, etc), go for fresh or dried as we've done, and adjust cooking times and methods accordingly, you're bound to achieve perfectly satisfactory results.

BRITISH & NORTH AMERICAN READERS:
Please note that Australian cup and spoon measurements are metric. A quick conversion guide appears on page 119. A glossary explaining unfamiliar terms and ingredients begins on page 113.

Opposite top Gingery fried bean-curd pouches with wasabi, page 18
Opposite below Lime-roasted spatchcock with noodles, page 66
Top Vietnamese beef noodle soup, page 10
Below Beef with sun-dried tomato sauce, page 42

Miso, laksa and other great soups

◄ When unexpected guests arrived, our parents used to joke that they'd "just throw another cup of water in the soup". Today, the expression should be amended to "just add noodles" because we've all come to appreciate what a satisfying extender they are. In this recipe selection, we've followed the Asian lead to create a line-up of soups which can be a meal on their own or part of a larger menu.

COCONUT SPINACH SOUP

Use either somyun, Korean wheat noodles, or somen, the Japanese version, for this recipe.

2 tablespoons vegetable oil
1 medium (150g) onion, chopped
2 cloves garlic, crushed
1 tablespoon chopped fresh ginger
1 tablespoon garam masala
1 teaspoon ground cardamom
1 teaspoon cumin seeds, crushed
1 teaspoon coriander seeds, crushed
2 bunches (1kg) English
   spinach, trimmed
2 large (600g) potatoes, chopped
2¹/₂ cups (625ml) chicken stock
1²/₃ cups (400ml) coconut cream
225g dried wheat noodles
1 cup (250ml) cream
2 tablespoons lime juice
¹/₄ cup (15g) shredded
   coconut, toasted

Heat oil in medium pan; cook onion, garlic, ginger, spices and seeds, stirring, until onion is soft. Add spinach and potatoes; stir until spinach is wilted. Stir in stock and coconut cream. Bring to boil; simmer, uncovered, 30 minutes.

Meanwhile, cook noodles in large pan of boiling water, uncovered, until just tender; drain. Cover to keep warm.

Blend or process spinach mixture, in batches, until smooth; return to pan. Stir in cream and juice; stir over heat, without boiling, until hot.

Divide noodles among serving bowls, ladle in hot soup; sprinkle with coconut.

SERVES 6 TO 8

Best made just before serving

MEATBALLS IN BROTH WITH GARLIC CROUTONS

Shanghai's cuisine responds to its long, cold winters: robust, nourishing noodles are the daily staple rather than rice in this wheat-growing region.

2 slices wholemeal bread
1 clove garlic, crushed
2 tablespoons vegetable oil
400g lean minced lamb
1¹/₂ tablespoons chopped fresh sage leaves
5 cloves garlic, crushed, extra
1 litre (4 cups) beef stock
2 cups (500ml) vegetable stock
1 tablespoon sugar
1¹/₂ tablespoons chopped fresh lemon grass
1 tablespoon finely grated lime rind
300g dried Shanghai noodles
100g enoki mushrooms
3 green onions, sliced

Discard crusts from bread; cut bread into 1cm pieces. Combine garlic and oil in medium bowl; toss bread until coated. Place bread in single layer on oven tray. Bake in moderate oven about 10 minutes or until croutons are browned and crisp.

Combine lamb, sage, and 3 cloves of the extra garlic in medium bowl. Roll heaped tablespoons of mixture into balls; place on tray. Cover; refrigerate 1 hour.

Heat stocks in large pan; add remaining extra garlic, sugar, lemon grass and rind. Bring to boil; simmer, uncovered, 5 minutes. Add meatballs and noodles to the stock mixture. Bring to boil; boil, uncovered, 4 minutes or until meatballs are cooked through. Divide mushrooms and onions among serving bowls. Ladle in hot broth with noodles and meatballs; scatter with croutons.

SERVES 4 TO 6

Meatballs can be prepared 1 day ahead

Storage Covered, in refrigerator
Freeze Uncooked meatballs suitable

⊏ **SHANGHAI NOODLES** are made from semolina, the coarsely-milled inner part of durum wheat; they are sold fresh, as a thick, spaghetti-type noodle, or dried, as a thin white noodle. Depending on the recipe, various kinds of fresh or dried wheat noodles could be substituted.

ROASTED TOMATO AND BORLOTTI BEAN SOUP

We used somen, a Japanese wheat noodle, but any thin noodle works well in this soup.

20 large (1.8kg) egg tomatoes, halved lengthways
1 teaspoon salt
1 teaspoon cracked black pepper
¹/₂ large (50g) garlic bulb
1 tablespoon olive oil
1 large (200g) onion, chopped
1.25 litres (5 cups) vegetable stock
¹/₄ cup loosely packed fresh basil leaves
1 tablespoon balsamic vinegar
1 teaspoon sugar
400g can borlotti beans, rinsed, drained
100g somen
2 tablespoons shredded fresh basil leaves, extra

Place tomatoes, cut side up, on wire racks over baking dishes, sprinkle with salt and pepper. Wrap unpeeled garlic bulb in foil, place on rack with tomatoes. Bake, uncovered, in moderate oven 1¹/₂ hours or until softened; cool. Squeeze garlic from skins; reserve pulp, discard skins.

Heat oil in large pan; cook stirring, until soft. Add tomatoes, pulp, stock, basil, vinegar and sugar. Br to boil; simmer, covered, 15 minutes.

Blend or process tomato mixture, in batches, until smooth. Return tomato mixture to pan with beans. Bring to boil, stirring, 2 minutes.

Meanwhile, cook noodles in medium pan of boiling water, uncovered, until just tender; drain.

Divide noodles among bowls. Ladle in hot soup; sprinkle with extra basil.

SERVES 6

Best made just before serving

Opposite Meatballs in broth with garlic croutons
Below Roasted tomato and borlotti bean soup

onion,
garlic
ring

THAI PUMPKIN SOUP

We used Jarrahdale pumpkin and mung bean thread noodles in this, our version of the traditional Thai favourite, gaeng lieng fak thong.

2 tablespoons peanut oil
1.5kg pumpkin, chopped
2 medium (240g) carrots, chopped
1 large (300g) potato, chopped
1 large (200g) onion, chopped
1.5 litres (6 cups) chicken stock
1 tablespoon sambal oelek
1¹/₂ tablespoons chopped
  fresh lemon grass
1 tablespoon lime juice
2 teaspoons garam masala
100g bean thread noodles
1 cup (250ml) coconut milk
¹/₄ cup (15g) shredded
  coconut, toasted
2 tablespoons fresh coriander leaves

Heat oil in large pan; cook pumpkin, carrot, potato and onion, stirring, until browned lightly. Stir in stock, sambal oelek, lemon grass, juice and garam masala. Bring to boil; simmer, uncovered, 30 minutes.

Meanwhile, cut noodles into 5cm lengths, place in medium heatproof bowl, cover with boiling water, stand until just tender; drain.

Blend or process mixture, in batches, until smooth; return to pan. Stir in milk and noodles. Bring to boil; simmer, stirring, 2 minutes.

Ladle hot soup into serving bowls; scatter with coconut and coriander.

SERVES 6 TO 8

Best made just before serving

COCONUT CHICKEN SOUP

Tom kha gai is a Thai soup that has made its way into our lives on a regular basis. Try our version, using fresh thin egg noodles.

1 litre (4 cups) chicken stock
1³/₄ cups (450ml) coconut milk
1/3 cup (80ml) lime juice
1/4 cup (60ml) fish sauce
1¹/₂ tablespoons finely chopped
    fresh lemon grass
6 kaffir lime leaves, torn
3 fresh coriander roots
1 teaspoon brown sugar
4 small fresh red chillies,
    seeded, sliced
2 large (340g) chicken breast
    fillets, sliced thinly
180g fresh egg noodles
1/3 cup loosely packed fresh
    coriander leaves

Add stock, milk, juice, sauce, lemon grass, lime leaves, coriander roots, sugar and half the chillies to large pan. Bring to boil; simmer, covered, 30 minutes. Discard coriander roots. Bring soup mixture to boil; stir in chicken and noodles. Bring to boil; simmer, covered, 1 minute. Ladle hot soup into serving bowls; sprinkle with coriander and remaining chilli.

SERVES 4

Best made just before serving

◻ **BEAN THREAD NOODLES** are sometimes known as cellophane or glass noodles because they are transparent when cooked, but are also well-known as bean thread vermicelli. Soak them only until they are soft — any longer and they become stodgy or start to fragment.

MISO SOUP

There are as many varieties of this clear Japanese soup as there are families in Japan. We used brown miso (also sold as brown soya bean paste) and mung bean thread noodles.

100g bean thread noodles
1/3 cup (80ml) brown miso
1.5 litres (6 cups) water
2¹/₂ teaspoons dashi granules
300g firm tofu, chopped
2 green onions, sliced
80g bean sprouts

Cut noodles into 5cm lengths. Place noodles in medium heatproof bowl, cover with boiling water, stand until just tender; drain.

Blend miso with 1 cup (250ml) of the water; strain into small jug.

Add remaining water to large pan with dashi; stir until dissolved. Add noodles; bring to boil then remove from heat. Stir in miso mixture; add tofu.

Divide onions and sprouts among serving bowls; ladle in hot soup.

SERVES 4 TO 6

Must be made just before serving

Opposite above   Thai pumpkin soup
Opposite below   Coconut chicken soup
Below   Miso soup

VIETNAMESE BEEF NOODLE SOUP

Pho bo is Vietnam's national dish, served at any time of day, both at home and by street vendors. Our version uses 1cm-wide fresh rice noodles, fresh banh pho. To slice beef into paper-thin pieces, cover with plastic wrap and freeze for 30 minutes or until just firm.

2 small fresh red chillies
1 tablespoon peanut oil
1 large (200g) onion, chopped
2 cloves garlic, crushed
1 medium (120g) carrot, chopped
1 tablespoon grated fresh ginger
1 litre (4 cups) beef stock
2 cups (500ml) water
1 teaspoon black peppercorns
2 star anise
1 tablespoon fish sauce
500g beef rump steak, sliced thinly
400g fresh rice noodles
120g bean sprouts
3 green onions, sliced thickly
2 tablespoons fresh mint leaves
1/2 medium (70g) lemon, quartered

Remove seeds and membranes from chillies; cut lengthways into thin strips.

Heat oil in large pan; cook onion, garlic, carrot and ginger, stirring, until onion is soft. Stir in stock, water, pepper, star anise and sauce. Bring to boil; simmer, uncovered, 30 minutes.

Strain stock mixture through 2 pieces of muslin into large pan; discard vegetables and muslin. Bring stock to boil.

Meanwhile, divide chilli, beef, noodles, sprouts, onions, mint and lemon among serving bowls; ladle in boiling stock.

SERVES 4

Vietnamese beef noodle soup must be made upon serving. Vegetable stock can be prepared 1 day ahead

Storage Covered, in refrigerator
Freeze Stock suitable

PRAWN LAKSA

This spicy Malaysian soup has become so commonplace that its name has made it into our everyday language. We used fresh thin egg noodles and dried rice stick noodles.

1kg large uncooked prawns
1 tablespoon vegetable oil
3¹/₄ cups (800ml) coconut milk
1 litre (4 cups) chicken stock
1¹/₂ tablespoons lime juice
3 teaspoons brown sugar
3 teaspoons fish sauce
6 kaffir lime leaves, torn
125g dried rice noodles
250g fresh egg noodles
80g bean sprouts
2 tablespoons fresh coriander leaves

LAKSA PASTE
2 teaspoons ground coriander
2 teaspoons ground cumin
1 teaspoon ground turmeric
1 large (200g) onion, chopped
¹/₃ cup (80ml) coconut milk
1 tablespoon grated fresh ginger
4 cloves garlic, crushed
¹/₄ cup (30g) finely chopped
   fresh lemon grass
2 small fresh red chillies,
   seeded, chopped
6 macadamias, chopped
1 tablespoon shrimp paste

Shell and devein prawns, leaving tails on.

Heat oil in large pan; cook Laksa Paste, stirring, until fragrant. Stir in milk, stock, juice, sugar, sauce and lime leaves. Bring to boil; simmer, covered, 30 minutes.

Place rice noodles in medium heatproof bowl, cover with boiling water, stand until just tender; drain.

Cook egg noodles in large pan of boiling water, uncovered, only until just tender; drain.

Stir prawns into soup mixture; simmer, uncovered, about 5 minutes or just until prawns change colour.

Just before serving, divide both noodles among serving bowls. Ladle in hot soup; top with sprouts and coriander.

Laksa Paste Blend or process all ingredients until smooth.

SERVES 4 TO 6

Prawn laksa must be made upon serving. Laksa paste can be prepared 3 days ahead

Storage Covered, tightly, in refrigerator
Freeze Laksa paste suitable

Opposite Vietnamese beef noodle soup
Right Prawn laksa

HOT AND SOUR SEAFOOD SOUP

The tangy Thai soup, tom yum goong, has become a firm favourite worldwide. We used a fresh wheat noodle traditionally made by hand in Asia but available ready-made here.

750g large uncooked prawns
250g firm white fish fillets
1 tablespoon peanut oil
1 large (200g) onion, sliced
6 green onions, chopped
4 cloves garlic, crushed
1 tablespoon grated fresh ginger
2 teaspoons sambal oelek
1 tablespoon finely chopped fresh lemon grass
2 kaffir lime leaves, torn
2 tablespoons tamarind concentrate
2 teaspoons sugar
2 tablespoons fish sauce
1 litre (4 cups) water
2 cups (500ml) chicken stock
2 tablespoons tomato paste
250g fresh wheat noodles
2 tablespoons shredded fresh coriander leaves
2 tablespoons shredded fresh mint leaves
20g bean sprouts

Shell and devein prawns. Cut fish into 2cm pieces.

Heat oil in large pan; cook both onions, garlic, ginger, sambal oelek, lemon grass and lime leaves, stirring, until onions are soft. Stir in tamarind, sugar, sauce, water, stock and paste; bring to boil.

Add noodles, return to boil; simmer, uncovered, 1 minute. Add herbs, prawns and fish; simmer, uncovered, about 3 minutes or until seafood is just cooked and noodles just tender.

Ladle soup into serving bowls; top with sprouts.

SERVES 4 TO 6

Best made just before serving

CHICKEN NOODLE SOUP

This Asian-influenced version of your homemade cold-remedy soup will inspire you. Try using the spaghetti-like fresh rice stick noodles to retain the soup's delicacy.

1.4kg chicken
3 litres (12 cups) cold water
1/2 teaspoon black peppercorns
1 celery stick, chopped
1 medium (350g) leek, chopped
2 kaffir lime leaves, torn
2 dried bay leaves
100g fresh coriander leaves, chopped
5cm piece (90g) fresh
    galangal, chopped
1 large (250g) corn cob, trimmed
125g fresh rice noodles

Combine chicken, water, pepper, celery, leek, all leaves and galangal in large pan. Bring to boil; simmer, uncovered, 50 minutes or until chicken is tender.

Remove chicken from pan; discard skin and bones. Shred chicken finely; cover to keep warm. Strain stock into large pan.

Cut kernels from corn; add to stock. Bring to boil; simmer, uncovered, 10 minutes or until stock is reduced by about a quarter.

Cook noodles in another large pan of boiling water, uncovered, until just tender; drain.

Divide chicken and noodles among serving bowls; ladle in hot soup.

SERVES 4 TO 6

Best made just before serving

◰ **FRESH RICE NOODLES**, also known as ho fun or fan in China and sen yai in Thailand, are the noodles upon which Vietnamese pho, Malaysian char kway teow and Thai pad seew have built their reputations. Fresh rice noodles are made daily in Asia and, at night, noodle vendors have a happy hour when remaining stock sells at a cheaper rate, as it can ferment if left overnight. Refrigerate these noodles and use as soon as possible after purchase.

HEARTY SICHUAN BEEF SOUP

Hokkien mee — fresh wheat noodles — are sold in most supermarkets these days.

1 teaspoon chopped fresh
    lemon grass
2 cloves garlic, crushed
2 teaspoons coriander seeds
1 1/2 teaspoons Sichuan pepper
500g whole piece beef rump steak
1 tablespoon sweet chilli sauce
2 tablespoons peanut oil
500g Hokkien mee
4cm piece fresh ginger, sliced thinly
2 litres (8 cups) beef stock
2 teaspoons ketjap manis
20g bean sprouts
1/4 cup fresh coriander leaves

Using a mortar and pestle (or a blender), crush lemon grass, garlic, seeds and pepper until almost smooth.

Combine spice mixture, beef, sauce and half the oil in medium bowl. Cover; refrigerate 3 hours or overnight.

Rinse noodles under hot water; drain. Transfer to large bowl; separate noodles with fork.

Cook beef on heated oiled griddle (or grill or barbecue) until browned both sides and cooked as desired. Slice beef thinly; cover to keep warm.

Heat remaining oil in large pan; cook ginger, stirring, until fragrant. Add stock and ketjap manis; bring to boil. Simmer; add noodles, stir until heated through.

Ladle hot soup into serving bowls; top with beef, sprouts and coriander.

SERVES 4 TO 6

Best made just before serving

Opposite above Hot and sour seafood soup
Opposite below Chicken noodle soup
Above Hearty Sichuan beef soup

MOROCCAN LAMB AND LENTIL SOUP

Harira, the Moroccan soup, is traditionally served as one of the dishes that breaks the daily fasting of the month-long Muslim observance of Ramadan. We added fresh thin egg noodles to further satisfy your hunger.

2 tablespoons olive oil
4 (800g) French-trimmed
   lamb shanks
2 medium (340g) red
   onions, chopped
3 cloves garlic, crushed
1 tablespoon ground cumin
1 teaspoon ground turmeric
2 teaspoons ground sweet paprika
1/4 teaspoon ground cinnamon
6 medium (1.1kg) tomatoes,
   peeled, seeded, chopped
2 x 300g cans chickpeas,
   rinsed, drained
1/3 cup (65g) red lentils,
   rinsed, drained
1.5 litres (6 cups) chicken stock
375g fresh egg noodles
2 tablespoons chopped fresh
   coriander leaves
1 1/2 tablespoons lemon juice

Heat oil in large pan; cook lamb until browned all over. Drain on absorbent paper. Cook onions, garlic and ground spices in same pan, stirring, 5 minutes. Return lamb to pan with tomatoes, chickpeas, lentils and stock. Bring to boil; simmer, covered, 2 hours or until lamb comes away from the bone, stirring occasionally. Remove lamb from pan; when cool enough to handle, pull lamb away from bones, discard bones. Chop lamb finely.

Cut noodles into 3cm lengths. Return lamb to pan; bring to boil. Add noodles, coriander and juice; boil, uncovered, until noodles are just tender.

SERVES 8

Best made just before serving

LONG AND SHORT SOUP

A favourite with many families, the combination of long noodles, a symbol of long life, and wontons, meat-filled dumplings in a clear broth, makes a meal in a bowl. We used dried rice stick noodles.

5 Chinese dried mushrooms
500g large uncooked prawns
1.5 litres (6 cups) chicken stock
1 cup (80g) shredded
**   Chinese cabbage**
¹⁄₄ cup (60ml) light soy sauce
¹⁄₄ cup (60ml) dry sherry
100g dried rice noodles
3 green onions, sliced
40g bean sprouts
1 tablespoon chopped fresh
**   coriander leaves**

WONTONS
50g chicken breast fillet, chopped
50g minced pork
1 clove garlic, crushed
1 teaspoon grated fresh ginger
1 tablespoon plum sauce
12 wonton wrappers
1 egg, beaten

Place mushrooms in small heatproof bowl, cover with boiling water, stand 20 minutes; drain. Discard stems; slice caps thinly. Shell and devein prawns, leaving tails intact.

Bring stock to boil in large pan. Add mushrooms, cabbage, sauce, sherry and Wontons; return to boil, then simmer, uncovered, 5 minutes. Add noodles and prawns; simmer until prawns change colour. Stir in remaining ingredients.

Wontons Blend or process chicken, pork, garlic, ginger and sauce until mixture forms a paste. Place rounded teaspoons of mixture in centre of wonton wrappers; brush edges lightly with egg. Bring opposite corners into centre of wonton wrapper, press along edges to seal.

SERVES 4

Long and short soup best made just before serving. Wonton filling and stock can be prepared 1 day ahead

Storage Covered, separately, in refrigerator

Opposite Moroccan lamb and lentil soup
Above Long and short soup

Just for starters

■ Whether you're after a curtain-raiser to the main course, finger food to serve at parties, or a range of delectable morsels to be accompanied by salad for a buffet lunch or supper, this bijou collection of recipes should satisfy most appetites and occasions. Noodles provide fabulous textures and the season's finest produce contributes a party of flavours to a stimulating celebration for the tastebuds.

VIETNAMESE RICE-PAPER ROLLS

These beautiful bites are a healthy alternative to the usual spring roll. Goi cuon are traditionally made with pork belly and prawns but we've gone for a lighter approach with chicken and mung bean thread noodles.

80g bean thread noodles
1 tablespoon peanut oil
600g chicken breast fillets
1/3 cup (80ml) peanut oil, extra
1 teaspoon sesame oil
1/3 cup (80ml) mirin
**2 tablespoons chopped fresh
    lemon grass**
2 teaspoons fish sauce
2 teaspoons ketjap manis
1 tablespoon chopped fresh ginger
2 cloves garlic, crushed
1/2 cup shredded fresh mint leaves
1 small (100g) red onion, sliced
**1/2 cup (70g) cashews,
    toasted, chopped**
80g bean sprouts
2 tablespoons grated lime rind
**4 small fresh red chillies,
    seeded, chopped**
16 x 22cm round rice paper sheets
16 fresh mint leaves
1/2 cup (125ml) mirin, extra
1/4 cup (60ml) ketjap manis, extra
1/3 cup (80ml) lime juice

Place noodles in small heatproof bowl, cover with boiling water, stand only until just tender; drain. Cut noodles into 4cm lengths.

Heat peanut oil in medium pan; cook chicken until tender and browned both sides. Cut chicken into thin slices.

Combine extra peanut oil, sesame oil, mirin, lemon grass, fish sauce, ketjap manis, ginger, garlic and mint in large bowl; stir in noodles, chicken, onion, cashews, sprouts, rind and chilli. Cover; refrigerate filling 30 minutes.

Place 1 sheet of rice paper in medium bowl of warm water until just softened; lift from water carefully, place on board. Place 1 mint leaf in centre of rice paper; top with 1 heaped tablespoon filling. Roll to enclose, folding in ends (roll should be about 8cm long). Repeat with remaining rice paper sheets, mint and filling.

Combine remaining extra mirin, extra ketjap manis and lime juice in small bowl; serve as a dipping sauce with rolls.

MAKES 16

Can be made 3 hours ahead

Storage Rice-paper rolls and sauce, covered, separately, in refrigerator

LION HEADS WITH BEAN-THREAD CRUNCH

We used mung bean thread noodles rather than grains of rice for the mane of our lions.

500g minced chicken
1/4 cup (35g) chopped pistachios, toasted
2 cloves garlic, crushed
2 teaspoons ground cumin
2 teaspoons grated lemon rind
130g can corn kernels, drained
1 cup (70g) stale breadcrumbs
1 egg, beaten
1/2 cup (75g) cornflour
1 egg, beaten, extra
1/2 cup (125ml) milk
200g bean thread noodles, crushed
vegetable oil, for deep-frying

ROAST CAPSICUM SAUCE
2 medium (400g) red capsicums
1/2 cup (125ml) cream
2 tablespoons coarsely grated parmesan cheese
1 clove garlic, chopped roughly

GINGERY FRIED BEAN-CURD POUCHES WITH WASABI

We used mung bean thread noodles in our version of this popular sushi snack.

80g bean thread noodles
1/3 cup seasoned rice vinegar
10 green onions
1/2 (65g) Lebanese cucumber
10 pouches prepared fried bean curd
30g pickled ginger, drained
2 teaspoons wasabi
1/4 cup (60ml) peanut oil
1/4 teaspoon sesame oil
1 teaspoon soy sauce
1/2 teaspoon sugar

Place noodles in large heatproof bowl, cover with boiling water, stand only until just tender; drain. Rinse under cold water; drain. Return noodles to same bowl; stir in half the vinegar. Line tray with plastic wrap, spread noodles on tray; cover, refrigerate until cold.

Meanwhile, cut green tops from onions to measure about 26cm in length. Place tops in small heatproof bowl, cover with boiling water, stand 5 minutes; drain. Rinse under cold water; drain.

Cut cucumber in thin, 5cm-long strips. Gently open out bean-curd pieces to form pouches. Divide noodles among pouches; divide cucumber, ginger and half the wasabi on top of noodles in pouches.

Tie onion tops around pouches to secure filling; trim ends of onion tops. Drizzle pouches with combined remaining vinegar and wasabi, both oils, sauce and sugar.

MAKES 10

Can be prepared 1 day ahead

Storage Covered, in refrigerator

Above Gingery fried bean-curd pouches with wasabi
Opposite above Sea scallops in black-bean sauce
Right Lion heads with bean-thread crunch

Combine chicken, nuts, garlic, cumin, rind, corn, breadcrumbs and egg in large bowl. Cover; refrigerate 1 hour.

Roll level tablespoons of chicken mixture into balls; toss in cornflour, shake off excess. Dip chicken balls in combined extra egg and milk; roll balls in noodles. Heat oil in large pan; deep-fry lion heads, in batches, until cooked through. Drain lion heads on absorbent paper; serve warm with Roast Capsicum Sauce.

Roast Capsicum Sauce Quarter capsicums, remove seeds and membranes. Roast capsicum pieces under grill or in very hot oven, skin-side up, until skin blisters and blackens. Wrap capsicum pieces in plastic or paper, 5 minutes; peel away skin.

Blend or process capsicums with cream, cheese and garlic until smooth. Transfer mixture to small pan; stir over heat until heated through.

MAKES 30

Lion heads can be prepared up to 3 hours before deep-frying. Roast capsicum sauce can be made 1 day ahead

Storage Covered, separately, in refrigerator
Freeze Sauce suitable

SEA SCALLOPS IN BLACK-BEAN SAUCE

Any dried rice noodle can be deep-fried for this recipe; we used a slightly wider variety so that the noodle pillows appear sturdy enough to support the scallops.

vegetable oil, for deep-frying
40g dried rice noodles
1 tablespoon salted black beans
2 teaspoons peanut oil
1 clove garlic, crushed
1 teaspoon grated fresh ginger
2 teaspoons salt-reduced soy sauce
2 teaspoons hoisin sauce
500g large white scallops
200g snow peas, sliced thinly
2 green onions, sliced thinly

Heat vegetable oil in large pan; deep-fry noodles, in batches, until puffed. Drain noodles on absorbent paper.

Rinse beans under cold water 1 minute; drain. Mash beans lightly . Heat peanut oil in wok or large pan; stir-fry beans, garlic and ginger until fragrant. Add sauces and scallops; stir-fry until scallops are just tender. Add peas; stir-fry 1 minute.

Divide noodles among serving plates; top with scallop mixture and onions.

SERVES 4

Best made just before serving

SALMON AND AVOCADO SUSHI

Our interpretation of that popular type of sushi known as a California roll is filled with green bean thread vermicelli rather than rice.

150g bean thread noodles
5 sheets toasted nori
100g sliced smoked salmon
1 medium (250g) avocado,
  sliced thinly
1 teaspoon rice vinegar
1 teaspoon sugar
2 teaspoons wasabi

Place noodles in large heatproof bowl, cover with boiling water, stand only until just tender; drain. Line tray with plastic wrap; spread noodles on tray. Cover; refrigerate until cold.

Place a sheet of nori, shiny-side down, with the long side towards you, on bamboo sushi mat. Spread one-fifth of the noodles over nori, leaving a 4cm border on far side.

Make hollow in centre of noodles; if noodles are too sticky, moisten fingers with a little rice vinegar.

Place one-fifth of the salmon and avocado in hollow as shown; brush with one-fifth of the combined vinegar, sugar and wasabi. Using bamboo mat as a guide, roll up nori from closest edge, pressing down firmly as you roll. Remove the mat carefully. Using sharp knife, trim edges, cut sushi roll into 6 pieces. Repeat with remaining ingredients.

MAKES 30

Salmon and avocado sushi can be made up to 30 minutes ahead

Storage Covered, in refrigerator

⊏ Nori is one of several kinds of seaweed used in Japanese cooking and, increasingly, our own. Today, it is possible to buy it already toasted and cut into the specific size needed for rolled sushi. Store it, airtight, in the freezer.

SANG CHOY BOW REVISITED

Here's a twist on the classic Chinese sang choy bow: we've provided fresh spinach leaves for wrapping the pork mixture in place of the traditional iceberg lettuce.

50g bean thread noodles
2 bunches (1kg) English spinach
1 tablespoon peanut oil
400g minced pork
2 cloves garlic, crushed
3 green onions, chopped
2 tablespoons light soy sauce
2¹/₂ tablespoons seasoned rice vinegar
3 teaspoons sambal oelek
¹/₂ teaspoon sesame oil
2 teaspoons grated lime rind
1¹/₂ tablespoons lime juice
2 tablespoons chopped fresh coriander leaves

Place noodles in small heatproof bowl, cover with boiling water, stand only until just tender; drain well. Cut noodles into 4cm lengths.

Trim and discard stems from spinach; wash well, pat dry.

Heat peanut oil in wok or large pan; stir-fry pork, garlic and onions until well browned. Add sauce, vinegar, sambal oelek, sesame oil, rind and juice; stir-fry 2 minutes. Stir in noodles and coriander.

Just before serving, place pork filling in bowl on serving platter; place spinach leaves around pork mixture. Each person spoons a little pork filling onto a spinach leaf then rolls leaf to enclose.

SERVES 8 TO 10

Best made on day of serving

Storage Covered, in refrigerator
Freeze Pork filling suitable

◧ **BEAN THREAD NOODLES** are called wun sen in Thailand and fun si in China. They look similar to vermicelli-type dried rice noodles but are tougher. They are quite hard to cut — use a cleaver but be very careful not to injure your hands. Better still, buy the kind that are sold tied in serving-sized bundles. Most recipes require them to be softened by soaking in boiling water for a few minutes. They can also be deep-fried to form puffed parcels.

Opposite Salmon and avocado sushi
Above Sang chow bow revisited

BUNDLES

*...also serve as an
...main courses. We
...wheat flour noodle,
...supple qualities.*

...0g udon
12 green onions

Cook noodles in large pan of boiling
water, uncovered, until just tender;
drain. Rinse under cold water; drain.
Spread noodles in thin layer on tray;
allow to cool.

Cut green tops from onions to
measure about 26cm in length. Place
tops in small heatproof bowl, cover
with boiling water, stand 5 minutes;
drain. Rinse under cold water; drain.

Shape noodles into 12 bundles; tie
with onion tops. Trim any loose bits
of noodles or onion tops.

MAKES 12

Best made on day of serving

Storage Covered, in refrigerator

LIME CHILLI SAUCE

*Both this sauce and the following one
can be used with any one of the three
recipes on this page or, indeed, all of
them. The noodle bundles, in particular,
are lovely eaten just as they are when
accompanied by this tart, tangy sauce.*

1 small fresh red chilli,
chopped finely
1/4 cup (60ml) lime juice
2 tablespoons brown sugar
1 tablespoon fish sauce
1 teaspoon finely chopped
fresh lemon grass

Combine ingredients in jar; shake well.

MAKES 1/2 CUP (125ML)

Can be made 1 day ahead

Storage Covered, in refrigerator

PEANUT CHILLI SAUCE

*Sweet chilli and peanut sauce is
associated with Thai food, and this one
goes really well with grilled meats.*

1/3 cup (80ml) sweet chilli sauce
1 tablespoon chopped
roasted peanuts
1 tablespoon chopped fresh
coriander leaves

Combine ingredients in jar; shake well.

MAKES 1/2 CUP (125ML)

Can be made 1 day ahead

Storage Covered, in refrigerator

CRISP PRAWNS

*Try this different coating when frying a
firm fish or chicken: crush a fine to
medium width mung bean noodle.*

18 (900g) medium
uncooked prawns
plain flour
1 egg, beaten
1/2 cup (125ml) milk
100g bean thread
noodles, crushed
1 tablespoon chopped fresh
coriander leaves
peanut oil, for deep-frying

Shell and devein prawns, leaving tails
intact. Toss prawns in flour; shake off
excess. Dip prawns in combined egg
and milk, then combined noodles and
coriander leaves.

Heat oil in large pan; deep-fry
prawns, in batches, until browned
and crisp. Drain prawns on sheets of
absorbent paper.

MAKES 18

Best made just before serving

RED CURRY NOODLE
PANCAKES

*Pancakes may be served room
temperature or hot. We used thin
rice vermicelli as part of the batter.*

80g dried rice noodles
2 green onions
1/2 cup (75g) plain flour
2 eggs, beaten
1/4 cup (60ml) coconut milk
1/4 cup (60ml) red curry paste
peanut oil, for shallow-frying

Place noodles in small heatproof
bowl, cover with boiling water, stand
until just tender; drain. Cut noodles
into 5cm lengths.

Remove and discard green tops of
onions; finely chop white portions.

Stir noodles and onions in medium
bowl with combined flour, eggs, milk
and paste.

Heat oil in large pan; shallow-fry
level tablespoons of mixture, in
batches, until browned and cooked
through. Drain on absorbent paper.

MAKES ABOUT 18

Can be prepared 3 hours ahead

Storage Covered, in refrigerator

Clockwise from top left Crisp prawns; Red
curry noodle pancakes; Peanut chilli
sauce; Lime chilli sauce; Noodle bundles

NOODLY CHICKEN SAMOSAS WITH PEANUT SAMBAL

We used green bean thread vermicelli inside these more-ish Indian snacks.

200g butternut pumpkin, chopped
1 medium (200g) potato, chopped
100g bean thread noodles
1 tablespoon vegetable oil
400g chicken breast fillets
1 medium (150g) onion, chopped
2 cloves garlic, crushed
2 teaspoons curry powder
6 sheets frozen ready-rolled puff
    pastry, thawed
1 egg, beaten
peanut oil, for deep-frying

PEANUT SAMBAL
8 green onions, chopped
3 small fresh red chillies,
    seeded, chopped
1/3 cup (80ml) lime juice
1 tablespoon peanut oil
11/3 cups (200g) unsalted
    roasted peanuts
12/3 cups (400ml) coconut milk
2 teaspoons tamarind concentrate
1/2 cup (125ml) water
1 tablespoon brown sugar

Boil, steam or microwave pumpkin and potato, separately, until tender; drain, mash together in large bowl.

Place noodles in medium heatproof bowl, cover with boiling water, stand until just tender; drain. Chop noodles coarsely; stir into mashed vegetables.

Heat vegetable oil in medium pan; cook chicken until tender. Chop chicken; add to noodle filling. Cook onion, garlic and curry powder in same pan, stirring, until onion is soft; add to noodle filling.

Using a 9.5cm cutter, cut 4 rounds from each pastry sheet. Place rounded tablespoons of noodle filling in centre of each round. Brush edges of pastry with a little egg; fold over, pinch edges firmly together to seal. Place samosas on tray, cover; refrigerate 1 hour.

Heat oil in large pan; deep-fry puffs, in batches, until heated through. Drain samosas on absorbent paper. Serve with Peanut Sambal.

Peanut Sambal Blend or process onions, chillies, juice, oil and peanuts until combined. Add combined remaining ingredients to medium pan; stir in peanut mixture. Bring mixture to boil; simmer, uncovered, about 4 minutes or until thickened slightly.

MAKES 24

Samosa filling and peanut sambal can be made 1 day ahead

Storage Covered, separately, in refrigerator
Freeze Uncooked samosas suitable

VEGETABLE AND RAMEN FRITTERS

Ramen, dried wheat noodles, are sometimes referred to as instant or 2-minute noodles in reference to their short cooking time. We used a straight version of ramen here.

100g ramen
1 tablespoon peanut oil
1 medium (150g) onion, chopped
2 cloves garlic, crushed
2 teaspoons grated fresh ginger
3 teaspoons black mustard seeds
3 teaspoons ground coriander
3 teaspoons ground cumin
1/2 teaspoon ground turmeric
1 medium (120g) carrot,
    grated coarsely
1 medium (200g) potato, grated
    coarsely, drained
1/2 cup (125ml) chicken stock
4 eggs, beaten
3/4 cup (180ml) yogurt
1 tablespoon lime juice
1 tablespoon chopped fresh mint
50g baby English spinach leaves
2 medium (380g) tomatoes, peeled,
    seeded, chopped

Cook noodles in large pan of boiling water, uncovered, until just tender; drain. Rinse under cold water; drain.

Heat oil in medium pan; cook onion, garlic and ginger, stirring, until onion is soft. Add seeds and spices; cook, stirring until seeds pop. Add carrot and potato; cook until soft, stirring occasionally. Stir in stock, bring to boil; simmer, uncovered, until almost all liquid evaporates. Cool.

Combine noodles and vegetable mixture in large bowl with eggs. Cook 1/3 cups of mixture in heated oiled medium non-stick pan, in batches, until browned both sides and cooked through.

Meanwhile, combine yogurt, juice and mint in small bowl. Serve yogurt sauce with fritters topped with spinach and tomatoes.

SERVES 4

Yogurt sauce can be prepared 1 day ahead

Storage Covered, in refrigerator

CHILLI CHICKEN PATTIES WITH LIME SAUCE

Any dried rice stick noodle can be crushed for the coating in this recipe; we chose to use a flat, fairly wide bean thread noodle.

50g dried rice noodles, crushed
750g minced chicken
2 teaspoons finely chopped fresh lemon grass
2 teaspoons chopped fresh red chilli
1 teaspoon finely grated lime rind
2 tablespoons chopped fresh coriander leaves
plain flour
2 tablespoons peanut oil
1/3 cup (80ml) lime juice
2 tablespoons fish sauce
2 tablespoons brown sugar
1/4 cup (60ml) dry white wine
1/3 cup (80ml) sweet chilli sauce

Place noodles in small heatproof bowl, cover with boiling water, stand until just tender; drain.

Combine noodles with chicken, lemon grass, chilli, rind and half the coriander in large bowl. Shape 1/4 cups of mixture into patties; toss in flour, shake off excess.

Heat oil in large pan; cook patties, in batches, until browned both sides and cooked through.

Combine remaining ingredients in jar; shake lime sauce well. Serve chicken patties with the lime sauce.

MAKES 14

Uncooked chilli chicken patties and sauce can be prepared 1 day ahead

Storage Covered, separately, in refrigerator
Freeze Uncooked patties suitable

◻ **RAMEN** is a crinkly or straight dried wheat noodle and a popular fast food in Japan where ramen bars are traditionally run by Chinese. Ramen was immortalised in the film *Tampopo* which tells the story of two truck drivers' quest to find the best ramen-maker in Japan. Sold in cakes, it is very popular in soups.

Opposite Noodly chicken samosas with peanut sambal
Above Vegetable and ramen fritters
Below Chilli chicken patties with lime sauce

MINI SPRING ROLLS WITH CHILLI CUCUMBER SAUCE

Thin wheat noodles, almost like vermicelli, make a surprise appearance in this recipe.

4 Chinese dried mushrooms
100g dried wheat noodles
1 clove garlic, crushed
1 teaspoon grated fresh ginger
4 green onions, sliced
1/2 medium (60g) carrot, sliced thinly
40g bean sprouts
2 teaspoons oyster sauce
2 teaspoons cornflour
2 teaspoons water
24 x 12.5cm square spring roll wrappers
peanut oil, for deep-frying

CHILLI CUCUMBER SAUCE
1 (130g) Lebanese cucumber, chopped finely
1/4 cup (60ml) sweet chilli sauce
1 small (130g) tomato, peeled, seeded, chopped
1 teaspoon light soy sauce
1 clove garlic, crushed

Place mushrooms in small heatproof bowl, cover with boiling water, allow to stand 20 minutes; drain. Discard stems; slice caps thinly.

Cook noodles in large pan of boiling water, uncovered, until just tender; drain. Rinse under cold water; drain. Cut noodles into 6cm lengths.

Combine mushrooms and noodles in large bowl with garlic, ginger, onions, carrot, sprouts and sauce. Blend cornflour with water in small bowl.

Spoon 1 level tablespoon of noodle mixture across a corner of one wrapper. Lightly brush edges of wrapper with a little cornflour mixture; roll to enclose filling, folding in ends. Roll should be 6cm long. Repeat with remaining noodle mixture, wrappers and cornflour mixture.

Just before serving, heat oil in large pan; deep-fry spring rolls, in batches, until golden brown and cooked through. Drain spring rolls on absorbent paper; serve with Chilli Cucumber Sauce.

Chilli Cucumber Sauce Reserve 1/4 cup cucumber. Blend or process remaining ingredients until smooth. Stir in reserved amount of cucumber.

MAKES 24

Filling and Chilli cucumber sauce can be made 3 hours ahead. Mini spring rolls can be prepared 30 minutes before deep-frying; cover with slightly damp tea-towel

Storage Covered, separately, in refrigerator
Freeze Uncooked rolls suitable

JAPANESE CHILLED NOODLES

Zaru-soba, a firm favourite in Japan's summers, is traditionally served on a bamboo mat fitted inside a tray or platter to allow any liquid to drain away from the noodles.

250g soba
2 sheets nori, toasted, shredded
2 green onions, chopped finely
1/4 cup (70g) pickled ginger
11/2 tablespoons wasabi

DIPPING SAUCE
1/2 cup (120ml) dark soy sauce
1/4 cup (60ml) mirin
1 teaspoon sugar
1/2 teaspoon dashi granules
11/4 cups (310ml) water
15g dried bonito flakes

Cook noodles in large pan of boiling water, uncovered, until just tender; drain. Rinse under cold water; drain. Cover; refrigerate at least 3 hours or until cold.

Divide noodles among 4 bamboo baskets; sprinkle with nori. Place onions, ginger, wasabi and Dipping Sauce in separate bowls; serve with noodles.

Dipping Sauce Combine sauce, mirin, sugar, dashi and water in medium pan. Bring to boil, add flakes; remove from heat. Strain into large bowl; discard flakes. Cover; refrigerate until cold.

SERVES 4

Best made on day of serving

◖ ZARU-SOBA is considered by many the connoisseur's soba as the merits of the noodles virtually stand alone. The origins of the name goes back 300 years, when soba was made by confectioners. Noodles made of 100% buckwheat broke easily, so the sweetmakers steamed and served them in take-zaru, bamboo baskets. Today, wheat flour is mixed with buckwheat to strengthen the noodles so they can be boiled, but the tradition of the bamboo basket remains, along with the name.

Below Mini spring rolls with chilli cucumber sauce
Opposite Japanese chilled noodles

STEAMED PORK DUMPLINGS
WITH PLUM SAUCE

Peking noodles were our choice for this classic pork and plum combination. You have to use noodles of the same length to achieve a neat result.

2 Chinese dried mushrooms
500g minced pork
2 green onions, chopped
2 cloves garlic, crushed
2 teaspoons grated fresh ginger
1¹/₂ cups (105g) stale breadcrumbs
2 tablespoons salt-reduced soy sauce
1 tablespoon hoisin sauce
1 egg, beaten
**2 tablespoons chopped fresh
   coriander leaves**
500g Peking noodles
600g choy sum, halved
¹/₂ cup (125ml) plum sauce
1 teaspoon sesame oil
¹/₃ cup (80ml) chicken stock
**1 tablespoon chopped fresh
   coriander leaves, extra**

Place mushrooms in small heatproof bowl, cover with boiling water, stand 20 minutes; drain. Discard stems; chop caps finely.

Combine mushrooms, pork, onion, garlic, ginger, breadcrumbs, sauces, egg and coriander in large bowl. Roll level tablespoons of pork mixture into dumplings; place on tray. Cover; refrigerate 30 minutes.

Place noodles in a single layer on work surface. Holding 5 or 6 noodles in your hand, wrap around each pork dumpling, as shown, finishing with noodle ends at the base.

Place dumplings, in single layer, about 2cm apart, in bamboo steamer lined with baking paper. Cook, covered, over wok or large pan of simmering water until dumplings are cooked through, brushing noodles with a little water occasionally.

Meanwhile, boil, steam or microwave choy sum until wilted; drain. Rinse under cold water; drain.

Combine remaining ingredients in small pan, stir plum sauce until heated through. Serve dumplings over choy sum with plum sauce.

SERVES 4 TO 6

Uncooked pork dumplings and plum sauce can be prepared 1 day ahead

Storage Covered, separately, in refrigerator
Microwave Plum sauce suitable

LAMB DOLMADES

Again, noodles replace rice in another traditional dish — this time, a Mediterranean favourite. We used extremely fine dried rice noodles here.

120g dried rice noodles, crushed
1 tablespoon olive oil
750g minced lamb
1 large (200g) onion, chopped
2 cloves garlic, crushed
2 teaspoons ground cumin
1/2 teaspoon grated lemon rind
1/4 cup (35g) plain flour
1/3 cup (80ml) water
200g vine leaves in brine

TOMATO SAUCE
1 tablespoon olive oil
1 large (200g) onion, chopped
1 clove garlic, crushed
2 x 400g cans tomatoes
**1 tablespoon chopped fresh
  mint leaves**

Place noodles in bowl, cover with boiling water, stand until just tender; drain.

Heat oil in large pan; cook lamb, stirring, until browned. Add onion and garlic; cook, stirring, until onion is soft. Stir in cumin, rind and flour; bring to boil, simmer, uncovered, about 10 minutes or until lamb mixture is thickened. Cool. Stir in noodles and water. Rinse vine leaves under cold water; drain, pat dry.

Place level tablespoons of lamb mixture in centre of each vine leaf. Fold in sides of leaf; roll up tightly to enclose filling. Place rolls close together in base of 2-litre (8-cup) ovenproof dish. Pour over Tomato Sauce; bake, covered, in moderate oven 30 minutes.

Tomato Sauce Heat oil in large pan; cook onion and garlic, stirring, until soft. Stir in undrained, crushed tomatoes and mint. Bring to boil; simmer, uncovered, about 10 minutes or until tomatoes are soft.

SERVES 4 TO 6
Lamb dolmades can be made 1 day ahead

Storage Covered, in refrigerator
Freeze Lamb mixture suitable

◱ **PEKING NOODLES** are a fresh wheat noodle, made without egg. These thin, rather square, camel-coloured noodles resemble the Italian pasta, linguine, and are extremely soft and malleable. They can be purchased in supermarkets and Asian food stores, fresh, in cryovac-packs.

Opposite Steamed pork dumplings with plum sauce
Below Lamb dolmades

Prime-time salads

■ Gone are the days of the salad as a bowl of tossed greens which, no matter how you dressed it up, smacked of deprivation. This round-up of recipes introduces the new-age salad as a stand-alone sensation, its delicious combinations guaranteed to turn even the most rabid salad-haters into aficionados. You'd make them just to taste but there's a bonus — they're good for you as well.

SMOKED SALMON, AVOCADO AND UDON SALAD

We used udon, the delectable wide, white, Japanese wheat noodle, in this light salad.

250g udon
300g sliced smoked salmon
90g snow pea sprouts
2 tablespoons chopped fresh chives
1 small (100g) red onion,
   chopped finely
2 small (450g) avocados,
   chopped finely
1/3 cup (80ml) light olive oil
2 tablespoons seasoned rice vinegar
1 tablespoon mirin
1 tablespoon lime juice
2 teaspoons wasabi

Cook noodles in large pan of boiling water, uncovered, until just tender; drain. Rinse under cold water; drain.

Separate smoked salmon slices; cut into small strips. Just before serving, gently toss noodles and salmon in large bowl with sprouts, chives, onion, avocados and combined remaining ingredients.

SERVES 4 TO 6

Best made just before serving

LEMON-MARINATED TUNA SALAD

We used banh pho, wide Vietnamese rice stick noodles, in this salad but you can use whichever dried rice noodle, whether Chinese, Thai or Taiwanese, you prefer.

500g piece fresh tuna fillet,
** split in half lengthways**
1/3 cup (80ml) olive oil
1 tablespoon grated lemon rind
1/2 cup (125ml) lemon juice
1 teaspoon cracked black pepper
2 cloves garlic, crushed
200g rice stick noodles
200g green beans
200g butter beans
1/3 cup (80ml) olive oil, extra
2 tablespoons chopped fresh parsley
1 medium radicchio, trimmed

Combine tuna, oil, rind, juice, pepper and garlic in large bowl; cover, refrigerate at least 3 hours or overnight.

Place noodles in large heatproof bowl, cover with boiling water, stand until just tender; drain. Rinse under cold water; drain. Boil, steam or microwave both beans until just tender; drain. Rinse under cold water; drain.

CHICKEN, CUCUMBER AND SPROUT SALAD

Locally manufactured fresh egg noodles, similar to tagliatelle, were used here.

11/4 cups (310ml) chicken stock
1/4 cup (60ml) lime juice
1/4 cup (60ml) dry white wine
3 (500g) chicken breast fillets
1 large (300g) cucumber
200g fresh egg noodles
120g bean sprouts
2 small fresh red chillies,
** seeded, sliced**
1 tablespoon chopped
** fresh coriander leaves**
1/4 cup (60ml) light olive oil
11/2 tablespoons lime juice, extra
1 tablespoon sweet chilli sauce
1 tablespoon seasoned rice vinegar
2 teaspoons hoisin sauce
1 teaspoon soy sauce

Combine stock, juice, wine and chicken in large pan. Bring to boil; simmer, covered, about 20 minutes or until chicken is just tender. Remove chicken from stock; when cool enough to handle, slice thinly.

Halve cucumber; remove seeds, slice diagonally. Cook noodles in large pan of boiling water, uncovered, until just tender; drain. Rinse under cold water; drain.

Gently toss chicken, cucumber and noodles in large bowl with bean sprouts, chillies, coriander leaves and combined remaining ingredients.

SERVES 6 TO 8

Can be prepared 1 day ahead

Storage Covered, in refrigerator
Microwave Chicken suitable

Above Chicken, cucumber and sprout salad
Right Lemon-marinated tuna salad
Opposite above Lime, tomato and scallop salad

Drain tuna; reserve marinade. Cook tuna in large heated oiled pan about 3 minutes each side or until browned but still pink inside. Remove from pan, cover; stand tuna 5 minutes. Cut into 1cm slices; cover to keep warm.

Transfer reserved marinade to same pan. Bring to boil; simmer, uncovered, 1 minute. Whisk in extra oil and parsley.

Gently toss tuna and noodles in large bowl with both beans, radicchio and warm marinade.

SERVES 4 TO 6

Lemon-marinated tuna salad best made just before serving. Tuna fillet can be marinated 1 day ahead

Storage Covered, in refrigerator
Microwave Beans suitable

◨ **RICE STICK NOODLES** only differ from dried rice noodles in that they are thicker. The two noodles can easily be interchanged with the only sacrifice being appearance in a dish such as pad thai which is traditionally made with the broader noodle. Soak to soften for about 4 to 8 minutes in boiling water before use. You might find them labelled ho fun on Chinese packets and sen lek in Thai.

LIME, TOMATO AND SCALLOP SALAD

The Thais use these ethereal rice stick noodles in their own cold noodle dishes.

250g dried rice noodles
500g large white scallops
1 tablespoon mild sweet chilli sauce
1 tablespoon lime juice
250g asparagus, trimmed, chopped
330g yellow teardrop tomatoes, halved
1/3 cup (25g) flaked almonds, toasted

LIME DRESSING
1/2 cup (125ml) peanut oil
1 teaspoon brown sugar
2 tablespoons chopped fresh coriander leaves
1 tablespoon chopped fresh mint leaves
2 small fresh red chillies, seeded
1/4 cup (60ml) lime juice

Place noodles in large heatproof bowl, cover with boiling water, stand only until just tender; drain. Rinse under cold water; drain.

Cook scallops, in batches, on heated oiled griddle (or grill or barbecue) until changed in colour, occasionally brushing with combined sauce and juice. Boil, steam or microwave asparagus until just tender; rinse under cold water, drain.

Gently toss noodles, scallops and asparagus in large bowl with tomatoes and Lime Dressing; sprinkle with almonds.

Lime Dressing Blend or process all ingredients until smooth.

SERVES 4

Best made just before serving

LAMB AND SPINACH SALAD

Beautiful Korean somyun noodles star here but you can substitute somen or even udon.

500g whole pieces lamb eye of loin
2 tablespoons green peppercorns, drained, chopped finely
1 tablespoon olive oil
250g cherry tomatoes, halved
150g dried wheat noodles
150g fetta cheese, chopped
250g baby English spinach leaves
1 clove garlic, chopped finely
1 teaspoon Dijon mustard
1/4 cup (60ml) white wine vinegar
1 tablespoon chopped fresh rosemary
1/2 cup (125ml) olive oil, extra

Roll lamb in green peppercorns. Heat 1 teaspoon of the oil in medium non-stick pan; cook lamb until browned all over and cooked as desired. Remove from pan, cover; stand 5 minutes. Cut into 1cm slices.

Place tomatoes in baking dish; drizzle with remaining oil. Bake, uncovered, in hot oven about 5 minutes or until just softened slightly.

Cook noodles in large pan of boiling water, uncovered, until just tender; drain. Rinse under cold water; drain.

Gently toss lamb, tomatoes and noodles in large bowl with fetta, spinach and combined remaining ingredients.

SERVES 4

Lamb and spinach salad best made just before serving. Lamb and tomatoes can be prepared 1 day ahead

Storage Covered, separately, in refrigerator

FETTA AND CAPSICUM SALAD

Hokkien mee is commonly thought of as the stir-fry noodle but here we eat it au naturel.

500g Hokkien mee
2 large (700g) red capsicums
4 medium (150g) egg tomatoes
1 tablespoon vegetable oil
150g fetta cheese
2 cups (300g) frozen broad beans, cooked, peeled
2 tablespoons fresh mint leaves, torn
1 small fresh red chilli, seeded, chopped finely
1 tablespoon chopped fresh coriander leaves
1 clove garlic, chopped finely
1 tablespoon lime juice
1 tablespoon balsamic vinegar
2 tablespoons sesame oil
2 tablespoons ketjap manis
2 teaspoons grated lime rind
2 teaspoons raw sugar

GRILLED VEGETABLE AND HALOUMI STACKS

Japanese soba come in many flavoured varieties (gozen soba), one of which is cha-soba, made with powdered green tea as well as buckwheat, the essential ingredient. Substitute cha-soba with any kind of soba you can find, or even a thin wheat noodle.

1 medium (300g) eggplant
coarse cooking salt
2 medium (400g) red capsicums
100g cha-soba
2 medium (240g) yellow
    zucchini, sliced
2 medium (240g) green
    zucchini, sliced
200g haloumi cheese, sliced
1/4 cup (60ml) olive oil
2 tablespoons balsamic vinegar
1 clove garlic, crushed
1 tablespoon chopped fresh oregano

Cut eggplant into 1cm slices, place on wire rack; sprinkle with salt, stand 30 minutes. Rinse slices under cold water; pat dry.

Quarter capsicums; remove seeds and membranes. Roast under grill or in very hot oven, skin-side up, until skin blisters and blackens. Wrap capsicum pieces in plastic or paper for 5 minutes, peel away skin; cut each quarter in half.

Cook noodles in large pan of boiling water, uncovered, until just tender; drain. Rinse under cold water; drain.

Cook capsicum and zucchini, on both sides, in batches, on heated oiled griddle (or grill or barbecue) until browned and just tender. Add cheese; cook, on both sides, about 30 seconds or until browned.

Stack vegetables, noodles and cheese on individual serving plates; drizzle with combined remaining ingredients.

SERVES 4

Best made just before serving

Rinse noodles under hot water; drain. Transfer to large bowl; separate noodles with a fork.

Quarter capsicums; remove seeds and membranes. Roast under grill or in very hot oven, skin-side up, until skin blisters and blackens. Wrap capsicum pieces in plastic or paper for 5 minutes, peel away skin; slice into thin strips.

Cut each tomato in half lengthways; place cut-side up on oven tray. Brush tomato halves with oil, grill 10 minutes or until browned and soft; cut each half into 2 wedges.

Cut cheese into 2cm cubes.

Just before serving, gently toss the noodles, capsicum strips, tomatoes and cheese in large bowl with beans, mint and combined remaining ingredients.

SERVES 4

Fetta and capsicum salad best made just before serving. Capsicum and tomatoes can be prepared 1 day ahead

Storage Covered, separately, in refrigerator

━ **STORAGE** Fresh noodles of all kinds should be refrigerated until required and used as soon as possible after purchase. Dried noodles have much longer lives. Provided they are stored in unopened packets or airtight containers, they can sit happily on the pantry shelf for several months.

Opposite above Lamb and spinach salad
Opposite Fetta and capsicum salad
Above Grilled vegetable and haloumi stacks

SESAME BEEF SALAD

The use of Dijon mustard and honey gives a unique lift to this classic Asian dish.

500g whole piece beef fillet steak
1 teaspoon grated fresh ginger
1 clove garlic, crushed
¹/₄ cup (60ml) light soy sauce
¹/₄ cup (60ml) sweet sherry
2 tablespoons sesame oil
250g asparagus, trimmed
150g snow peas, trimmed
250g dried wheat noodles
1 teaspoon Dijon mustard
2 teaspoons honey
1 tablespoon white wine vinegar
2 tablespoons olive oil
3 green onions, sliced
1 tablespoon sesame seeds, toasted

Combine beef with ginger, garlic, sauce, sherry and sesame oil in large bowl. Cover; refrigerate 3 hours or overnight.

Cut asparagus into 4cm lengths. Boil, steam or microwave asparagus and snow peas, separately, until just tender; drain. Rinse under cold water; drain.

HAZELNUT CHICKEN SALAD

The Chinese dried wheat noodle used here is labelled yolk noodle but, as is often the case with packaging translations, we suspect the pale yolky hue can be attributed more to food colouring than to an egg.

4 (680g) chicken breast fillets
1 clove garlic, crushed
1 tablespoon lime juice
2 tablespoons olive oil
170g dried wheat noodles
120g rocket, trimmed
200g curly endive, trimmed
¹/₂ cup (60g) hazelnuts,
  toasted, chopped
¹/₄ cup (60ml) raspberry vinegar
1 tablespoon seeded mustard
¹/₂ cup (125ml) hazelnut oil

Combine chicken, garlic, juice and olive oil in large bowl. Cover; refrigerate 3 hours or overnight.

Cook chicken on heated oiled griddle (or grill or barbecue) until browned both sides and tender. Remove from pan; slice into 2cm strips.

Cook noodles in large pan of boiling water, uncovered, until just tender; drain. Rinse under cold water; drain.

Gently toss chicken and noodles in large bowl with rocket, endive, nuts and combined remaining ingredients.

SERVES 4 TO 6

Hazelnut chicken salad best made just before serving. Chicken can be prepared 1 day ahead

Storage Covered, in refrigerator
Freeze Chicken suitable

Cook noodles in large pan of boiling water, uncovered, until just tender; drain. Rinse under cold water; drain.

Drain beef; reserve marinade. Cook beef in large heated oiled pan until browned both sides and cooked as desired. Remove from pan; slice beef thinly. Add marinade to same pan. Bring to boil; simmer, uncovered, about 2 minutes or until mixture thickens slightly.

Cool marinade then combine with mustard, honey, vinegar and olive oil in large bowl.

Just before serving, gently toss beef, asparagus, snow peas and noodles in large bowl with marinade mixture, onions and sesame seeds.

SERVES 4

Can be prepared 1 day ahead

Storage Covered, separately, in refrigerator

Opposite Hazelnut chicken salad
Below Sesame beef salad
Right Stringhopper salad

STRINGHOPPER SALAD

Stringhoppers are sometimes called Idly in Indian restaurants; look for them, dried, in both Indian and Sri Lankan shops.

1 tablespoon seasoned pepper
1kg whole piece beef rump steak
4 bacon rashers, chopped
vegetable oil, for deep-frying
80g dried stringhoppers
4 hard-boiled eggs, quartered
150g baby English spinach leaves
250g cherry tomatoes, halved
250g yellow tear-drop tomatoes, halved

ANCHOVY DRESSING
6 canned anchovy fillets, drained
1 clove garlic, crushed
2 teaspoons Dijon mustard
2 teaspoons white wine vinegar
1 teaspoon sugar
1/2 cup (125ml) olive oil
1/2 cup (125ml) buttermilk

Sprinkle pepper over beef. Cook beef on heated oiled griddle (or grill or barbecue) until browned both sides and cooked as desired. Remove from pan; cover. Stand 5 minutes; slice thinly.

Add bacon to same heated pan; cook, stirring, until crisp. Remove from pan; drain on absorbent paper.

Heat oil in large pan; deep-fry stringhoppers, in batches, until puffed. Drain stringhoppers on absorbent paper.

Gently toss beef and bacon in large bowl with eggs, spinach and tomatoes. Divide stringhoppers among 6 serving plates, top with beef mixture; drizzle with Anchovy Dressing.

Anchovy Dressing Blend or process anchovies, garlic, mustard, vinegar and sugar until almost smooth. With motor operating, gradually pour in oil; process until thick. Add buttermilk; process until thickened slightly.

SERVES 6

Best made just before serving

SWEET CHILLI PRAWN SALAD

Bean thread noodles are sometimes known as cellophane or glass noodles because of their fragile, transparent appearance.

vegetable oil, for deep-frying
80g bean thread noodles
16 (800g) medium
  uncooked prawns
2 tablespoons sesame oil
2 cloves garlic, crushed
3 green onions, chopped
80g bean sprouts
1 small (150g) red capsicum,
  seeded, sliced
30g snow peas, sliced finely

SWEET CHILLI SAUCE

6 small fresh red chillies,
  seeded, chopped
1 tablespoon sultanas
1 clove garlic, crushed
1 teaspoon grated fresh ginger
1 tablespoon white vinegar
1/4 cup (55g) sugar
1/2 teaspoon salt
1/4 cup (60ml) water

Heat oil in large pan; deep-fry noodles, in batches, until puffed. Drain noodles on absorbent paper.

Shell and devein prawns, leaving tails intact. Heat sesame oil in wok or large pan; stir-fry garlic, onions, sprouts, capsicum, snow peas and prawns until prawns are tender and change colour.

Just before serving, gently toss prawn mixture and noodles in large bowl with Sweet Chilli Sauce.

Sweet Chilli Sauce Blend or process all ingredients until well combined; transfer to small pan. Bring to boil; simmer, uncovered, until sauce thickens slightly, stirring occasionally.

SERVES 4

Best made just before serving

◰ **NOODLES** can replace rice, potatoes and other pastas in many of your favourite recipes, whether they're Asian in origin or not. Be daring, creative and ingenious with your cooking, and — who knows — one of your inventions could become a family favourite you make time and time again. And the world won't stop if one doesn't turn out to be perfect.

CRUNCHY COLESLAW WITH FRIED NOODLES

The fried noodles called for here are already prepared as crunchy dried egg noodles and are sold in 100g cellophane bags.

600g savoy cabbage, shredded
4 green onions, chopped finely
2 celery sticks, sliced finely
100g radishes, sliced finely
1 medium (120g) carrot,
**   sliced finely**
50g snow pea sprouts
1 tablespoon sesame seeds, toasted
200g fried noodles
1/2 cup (125ml) peanut oil
2 tablespoons cider vinegar
1/4 cup (50g) firmly packed
**   brown sugar**
2 teaspoons soy sauce
1/2 teaspoon sesame oil
1 clove garlic, crushed

Just before serving, gently toss cabbage, onions, celery, radishes, carrot, sprouts, seeds, noodles and combined remaining ingredients in large bowl.

SERVES 6 TO 8

Best made just before serving

CHAR-GRILLED CHILLI SQUID WITH RIBBON VEGETABLES

The fresh Hokkien mee you buy packaged at the supermarket needs no pre-cooking; just rinse under or submerge in hot water to help separate and loosen the strands.

1kg squid hoods, cleaned
2 tablespoons lime juice
1 teaspoon fish sauce
1/2 cup (125ml) sweet chilli sauce
2 tablespoons chopped fresh
**   coriander leaves**
500g Hokkien mee
1 medium (120g) carrot
1 medium (120g) green zucchini
1 medium (120g) yellow zucchini
1 medium (200g) red capsicum
1 tablespoon white vinegar
2 tablespoons lime juice, extra
1 teaspoon sugar
1/2 cup (125ml) olive oil
1 tablespoon chopped fresh
**   coriander leaves, extra**

Halve squid hoods; score shallow in criss-cross pattern on inside surface, cut into 3cm pieces. Mix squid with combined juice, sauces and coriander in large bowl. Cover; refrigerate 3 hours or overnight.

Rinse noodles under hot water; drain. Transfer to large bowl; separate noodles with a fork.

Drain squid; discard marinade. Cook squid, in batches, on heated oiled griddle (or grill or barbecue) until just cooked and curled.

Using a vegetable peeler, finely slice carrot and both zucchini into paper-thin ribbons. Quarter capsicum; remove and discard seeds and membranes. Using a sharp knife, cut capsicum into extremely thin strips.

Just before serving, gently toss the cooled squid, noodles and vegetable ribbons in large bowl with combined remaining ingredients.

SERVES 4 TO 6
Squid best prepared 1 day ahead

Storage Covered, in refrigerator

Opposite above Sweet chilli prawn salad
Opposite Crunchy coleslaw with
fried noodles
Above Char-grilled chilli squid with
ribbon vegetables

FRESH CRAB AND SMOKED SALMON SPRINGTIME SALAD

Bean thread noodles must only be soaked long enough to just soften them: too long and they become stodgy and can break up.

100g bean thread noodles
250g asparagus
200g snow peas, thinly sliced
100g sliced smoked salmon
250g shredded fresh crab meat
1 small (130g) cucumber,
  thinly sliced
4 green onions, sliced finely
1/2 cup (125ml) olive oil
1/4 cup (60ml) lemon juice
1 teaspoon finely grated lemon rind
1 clove garlic, crushed finely
1 teaspoon Dijon mustard
2 teaspoons finely chopped fresh dill

Place noodles in medium heatproof bowl, cover with boiling water, stand only until just tender; drain.

Snap off and discard tough ends of asparagus; cut spears in half. Boil, steam or microwave asparagus and snow peas, separately, until just tender; drain. Rinse under cold water; drain.

Separate salmon slices; cut into 1cm strips. Gently toss noodles, asparagus, snow peas, salmon, crab, cucumber and onions in large bowl with combined remaining ingredients.

SERVES 4 TO 6

Best made just before serving

PEKING DUCK SALAD

The delicate pancakes traditionally served with the first course of a Peking duck banquet are replaced by fine, fresh egg noodles in this main-course salad.

4 (950g) duck breast fillets
1/3 cup (80ml) hoisin sauce
250g fresh egg noodles
1 small (130g) cucumber, seeded, cut into 5mm slices
2 green onions, sliced
75g snow pea sprouts
2 tablespoons hoisin sauce, extra
1 tablespoon plum sauce
2 tablespoons rice vinegar
1/4 cup (60ml) peanut oil

Place duck in large baking dish; brush with hoisin sauce. Bake, uncovered, in moderate oven about 45 minutes or until cooked. Remove from pan; discard fat. When cool, cut into 5mm slices.

Cook noodles in large pan of boiling water, uncovered, until just tender; drain. Rinse under cold water; drain.

Just before serving, gently toss duck and noodles in large bowl with cucumber, onions, bean sprouts and combined remaining ingredients.

SERVES 4 TO 6

Peking duck salad best made just before serving. Duck breast fillets can be baked 1 day ahead

Storage Covered, in refrigerator
Freeze Duck breast fillets suitable

⌐ **WE HAVE TRIED** to be as specific as possible when it came to describing the noodle used in each recipe. However, if you can't find the specific noodle called for in the recipe, it's fine to substitute a variety which requires similar preparation and approximately the same cooking time. As long as you stay within the same basic ingredient family — wheat flour, rice flour, etc — and use a dried or fresh variety as called for, you're on the right track to success.

Meat
with the works

In keeping with the health-conscious mood of our times we've learned the value of quality rather than quantity and adjusted our butcher's orders accordingly. We've also tempered some of our favourite recipes by adding that other completely soul-nourishing staple — noodles. Here, lamb, beef, pork and veal star in a globetrotting array of dishes.

BEEF WITH SUN-DRIED TOMATO SAUCE

Any thin fresh noodle will work well with this lusciously rich sauce.

8 sun-dried tomatoes in
    oil, undrained
2 tablespoons balsamic vinegar
750g whole piece beef eye fillet
60g butter, softened
1 clove garlic, crushed
1/2 teaspoon sambal oelek
375g fresh egg noodles
2 tablespoons shredded
    fresh basil leaves

Drain tomatoes over small measuring jug; reserve oil. (Add enough olive oil to jug to make 1/4 cup.) Finely chop tomatoes.

Combine oil and vinegar in jar; shake vinaigrette well.

Coat piece of beef with 2 tablespoons of the vinaigrette in large bowl. Cook beef on heated oiled griddle (or grill or barbecue) until browned all over and cooked as desired. Remove beef, cover; stand 10 minutes. Slice beef thinly; cover to keep warm.

Combine butter, garlic, sambal oelek and half the tomatoes in small bowl.

Just before serving, cook noodles in large pan of boiling water, uncovered, until just tender; drain.

Gently toss hot noodles and basil in large bowl with butter mixture until butter is melted. Top noodle mixture with beef. Sprinkle with remaining tomatoes; drizzle with remaining vinaigrette.

SERVES 4 TO 6

Best made just before serving

PORK AND VEAL KOFTA

Soak bamboo skewers in water for 1 hour to prevent them scorching. If fresh chow mein are unavailable, try using an extremely thin fresh egg noodle instead.

1kg pork and veal mince
1 tablespoon ground cumin
2 cloves garlic, crushed
1 small (80g) onion, chopped finely
1/4 cup (35g) finely chopped dried apricots
1 tablespoon chopped fresh coriander leaves
1/4 cup (35g) slivered almonds, toasted, chopped
1 teaspoon hot paprika
180g fresh chow mein, chopped
1 egg, beaten
3/4 cup (180ml) yogurt
1 tablespoon chopped fresh mint leaves
1 teaspoon ground cumin, extra
1 teaspoon sugar

Combine mince, cumin, garlic, onion, apricots, coriander, almonds, paprika, noodles and egg in large bowl. Cover; refrigerate 30 minutes. Roll level tablespoons of mixture into oval-shaped kofta; thread 3 kofta onto each skewer.

Cook kofta, in batches, on heated oiled griddle (or grill or barbecue), until browned and cooked through.

Combine yogurt, mint, extra cumin and sugar in small bowl.

Serve kofta with yogurt sauce.

SERVES 4 TO 6

Kofta and yogurt sauce can be prepared 1 day ahead

Storage Covered, separately, in refrigerator
Freeze Kofta suitable

WHILE IT'S fine to make substitutions when cooking with noodles, read the contents' description on the package to make sure you're substituting a similar kind of noodle. Some labels can be very misleading, as for example, some noodles described as egg don't contain any but are simply an egg-yolk yellow in colour; another package might be called fresh egg, when in fact, it's a dried noodle to which a "fresh egg" was added during the manufacturing process.

Above left Pork and veal kofta
Left Mustard-curry pork slices in mushroom sauce
Opposite Lamb with garlic noodles

LAMB WITH GARLIC NOODLES

We used Japanese udon here and suggest you do, too, if this wholesome wheat noodle is available in your area. You will use 1/3 cup (80ml) of garlic mayonnaise here; store the remainder in a tightly sealed jar, the surface covered with a little olive oil, under refrigeration for 1 day. Use the remaining sauce in a dressing for a green salad.

500g whole pieces lamb eye of loin
2 teaspoons cracked black pepper
1 tablespoon finely grated
  lemon rind
1/2 cup (125ml) olive oil
250g udon
1 tablespoon cider vinegar
250g cherry tomatoes, halved
1/4 cup fresh basil leaves
vegetable oil, for deep-frying
1 large (200g) onion, sliced thinly

GARLIC MAYONNAISE
1 medium bulb (70g) garlic, peeled,
  chopped coarsely
1 egg yolk
2 teaspoons water
2 tablespoons lemon juice
1 cup (250ml) olive oil

Combine lamb pieces, pepper, rind and 2 tablespoons of the olive oil in a large bowl. Cover lamb; refrigerate 3 hours or overnight.

Cook lamb on heated oiled griddle (or grill or barbecue) until browned all over and cooked as desired. Remove lamb, cover; stand 10 minutes. Slice lamb thinly; cover to keep warm.

Cook noodles in large pan of boiling water, uncovered, until just tender; drain.

Combine remaining olive oil, vinegar and 1 teaspoon of the Garlic Mayonnaise in jar; shake vinaigrette well. Gently toss lamb, noodles, tomatoes and basil with vinaigrette in large bowl.

Heat vegetable oil in large pan; deep-fry onion rings, in batches, until browned and crisp. Drain onion rings on absorbent paper. Top noodles and lamb with onion rings and the remainder of the 1/3 cup of the Garlic Mayonnaise.

Garlic Mayonnaise Blend or process garlic, egg yolk, water and juice until combined. With motor operating, gradually pour in oil; process until thick.

SERVES 4

Lamb with garlic noodles best made just before serving. Lamb and garlic mayonnaise can be prepared 1 day ahead

Storage Covered, separately, in refrigerator

MUSTARD-CURRY PORK SLICES IN MUSHROOM SAUCE

Any dried noodle can be used here but we liked it best with these flat dried wheat noodles.

2 teaspoons mild curry powder
1 tablespoon seeded mustard
2 (480g) pork fillets
1 tablespoon olive oil
1 large (200g) onion, sliced
1 clove garlic, crushed
250g button mushrooms, sliced
1/4 cup (60ml) dry white wine
2 tablespoons Dijon mustard
1 cup (250ml) cream
1/4 cup (60ml) water
250g dried wheat noodles
1 tablespoon chopped fresh parsley

Spread combined curry powder and seeded mustard over pork; place in oiled baking dish. Bake, uncovered, in moderate oven about 30 minutes or until cooked as desired. Remove pork, cover; stand 10 minutes. Slice pork thinly; cover to keep warm.

Heat oil in medium pan; cook onion and garlic, stirring, until onion is soft. Add mushrooms; cook, stirring, until just tender. Stir in wine. Bring to boil; simmer until almost all liquid evaporates. Stir in Dijon mustard with cream and water; cook, stirring until heated through.

Meanwhile, cook noodles in large pan of boiling water, uncovered, until just tender; drain.

Gently toss noodles with pork and mushroom sauce in large bowl; sprinkle with parsley.

SERVES 4 TO 6

Best made just before serving

SUKIYAKI

Perhaps Japan's most well-known dish, sukiyaki is easy to make at home — and it makes a fabulous dinner party main course: simply double the quantities below to feed 8 people. While a traditional sukiyaki pan can be purchased from Japanese or Asian kitchen shops, your electric frypan is a good substitute for table-top cooking. Only a small quantity of sukiyaki is cooked at a time to ensure the vegetables are not overdone. Each guest has their own bowl which, traditionally, has a broken raw egg in it: the first spoonful of hot sukiyaki cooks the egg.

- 8 **Chinese dried mushrooms**
- 2 **green onions, chopped**
- 1 **small (150g) green capsicum, seeded, sliced**
- 1/4 **small (200g) Chinese cabbage, chopped**
- 1 **bunch (500g) English spinach, trimmed**
- 160g **bean sprouts**
- 75g **shirataki noodles**
- 400g **whole piece beef eye fillet, sliced thinly**
- 300g **packet firm tofu, chopped**
- 2 **tablespoons peanut oil**
- 4 **eggs**

MIRIN SAUCE
- 1/2 **cup (125ml) light soy sauce**
- 1/2 **cup (125ml) water**
- 1/4 **cup (60ml) dark soy sauce**
- 1/4 **cup (60ml) mirin**
- 1/4 **cup (55g) sugar**
- 1 **teaspoon dashi granules**

Place mushrooms in small heatproof bowl, cover with boiling water, stand 20 minutes; drain. Discard stems; slice caps. Arrange vegetables, sprouts, noodles, beef and tofu on platter.

In a sukiyaki pan (or electric frypan) at the table, heat 2 teaspoons of the oil; stir-fry a quarter of the beef and onions until just cooked. Add a quarter of the mushrooms, capsicum, cabbage, spinach, noodles and tofu to pan; stir-fry until just cooked. Add a quarter of the sprouts and Mirin Sauce; cook 30 seconds. Serve immediately in individual bowls. Repeat with remaining ingredients.

Mirin Sauce Stir all ingredients in medium pan over low heat until sugar dissolves; simmer gently 10 minutes.

SERVES 4

Sukiyaki ingredients can be prepared 3 hours ahead. Mirin sauce can be made 1 day ahead

Storage Covered, separately, in refrigerator

LAMB WITH ROASTED TOMATOES AND WALNUTS

You can use any fresh noodle you like in this recipe since they're not cooked with the meat; here we used Hokkien mee.

- 2 x 350g **whole pieces lamb eye of loin**
- 2 **tablespoons balsamic vinegar**
- 2 **tablespoons lemon juice**
- 1/4 **cup (60ml) olive oil**
- 1 **tablespoon chopped fresh rosemary**
- 2 **teaspoons brown sugar**
- 8 **medium (600g) egg tomatoes, quartered lengthways**
- 1 **teaspoon salt**
- 1 **teaspoon cracked black pepper**
- 1 **small (50g) whole garlic bulb**
- 600g **Hokkien mee**
- 125g **baby English spinach leaves**
- 3/4 **cup (75g) walnuts, toasted**

Combine lamb pieces, vinegar, juice, oil, rosemary and sugar in large bowl. Cover; refrigerate 3 hours or overnight.

Place tomatoes, cut-side up, on wire rack over baking dish; sprinkle with salt and pepper. Wrap garlic in foil, place on rack with tomatoes. Bake, uncovered, in moderate oven about 1 hour or until tomatoes and garlic are very soft. When cool enough to handle, peel garlic; reserve pulp.

Drain lamb over large bowl; reserve marinade. Cook lamb on heated oiled griddle (or grill or barbecue) until browned both sides and cooked as desired. Remove lamb, cover; stand 10 minutes. Slice lamb thinly; cover to keep warm.

Rinse noodles under hot water; drain. Transfer to large bowl; separate noodles with a fork.

Place reserved marinade in small pan; boil 1 minute. Stir in garlic pulp.

Gently toss hot noodles with spinach, walnuts, lamb and hot marinade in large bowl. Add tomatoes; toss gently.

SERVES 4 TO 6

Lamb with roasted tomatoes and walnuts must be made just before serving. Lamb best marinated 1 day ahead

Storage Covered, in refrigerator

☐ **SHIRATAKI** The translation of the Japanese name as "white waterfall" rather romantically describes these transparent thin noodles which are sold both dried and fresh in water packs. They are made from a root vegetable called konnyaku, meaning "devil's tongue" which is also how they are sometimes labelled. Dried shirataki need to be softened by soaking in hot water for a few minutes before adding to dishes such as sukiyaki. Bean thread noodles could be substituted if shirataki are unavailable.

Opposite Sukiyaki
Above Lamb with roasted tomatoes and walnuts

CHINESE ROAST PORK WITH STACKED NOODLE OMELETTES

This impressive dish uses mung bean thread noodles in the omelettes but you can substitute a fine fresh egg noodle if you like — but remember to alter the noodle's cooking time accordingly.

**1/4 cup (60ml) salt-reduced
  soy sauce**
2 tablespoons black bean sauce
1 clove garlic, crushed
2 teaspoons grated fresh ginger
3 (720g) pork fillets
125g bean thread noodles
10 eggs, beaten
3 green onions, sliced thinly
2 tablespoons peanut oil
BLACK BEAN SAUCE
3 teaspoons cornflour
1 cup (250ml) chicken stock
1/4 cup (60ml) black bean sauce
1/4 teaspoon sesame oil

Spread combined sauces, garlic and ginger over pork in shallow dish. Cover; refrigerate 3 hours or overnight. Remove pork from marinade; discard marinade.

Place pork on wire rack in baking dish; bake, uncovered, in moderately hot oven 30 minutes or until pork is cooked as desired, brushing occasionally with pan juices. Remove pork from oven, cover; stand 10 minutes. Slice pork thinly; cover to keep warm.

Place noodles in medium heatproof bowl, cover with boiling water, stand until just tender; drain. Cut noodles into small pieces over large bowl; whisk in eggs and onion.

Brush 20cm heavy-based pan with some of the peanut oil; heat pan. Pour in 1/4 cup omelette mixture; cook, un-covered, until set underneath. Turn, cook other side. Place omelette on sheet of baking paper. Repeat with remaining oil and omelette mixture, layering cooked omelettes between separate pieces of baking paper. You need 12 omelettes.

Place 1 omelette on each of 4 serving plates, top with some of the pork, then another omelette and more pork, topping each stack with a third omelette. Drizzle with Black Bean Sauce before serving.

Black Bean Sauce Blend cornflour with a little stock in small pan; gradually stir in remaining stock, sauce and oil. Stir over heat until mixture boils and thickens.

SERVES 4

Omelettes best made just before serving. Pork can be marinated 1 day ahead. Black bean sauce can be made 1 day ahead

Storage Covered, separately, in refrigerator

SINGAPORE NOODLES

This combination of pork, prawns and thin fresh egg noodles will help conjure visions of a meal in a Singaporean night market.

10 Chinese dried mushrooms
450g fresh egg noodles
2 tablespoons peanut oil
5 cloves garlic, crushed
1 tablespoon grated fresh ginger
2 tablespoons curry paste
**230g can water chestnuts,
  drained, chopped**
4 green onions, chopped
200g Chinese barbecue pork, sliced
**400g medium uncooked prawns,
  shelled, deveined**
2 tablespoons light soy sauce
2 tablespoons oyster sauce
2 tablespoons dry sherry
3 eggs, beaten
2 teaspoons sesame oil

Place mushrooms in small heatproof bowl, cover with boiling water, stand 20 minutes; drain. Discard stems; chop caps finely.

Rinse noodles under cold water; drain.

Heat peanut oil in wok or large pan; stir-fry garlic, ginger and paste about 2 minutes or until fragrant. Add mushrooms, chestnuts, onion and pork; stir-fry about 2 minutes or until chestnuts are browned lightly. Add prawns; stir-fry until prawns change colour. Add noodles and combined sauces and sherry; stir-fry until most of the liquid is absorbed. Add combined eggs and sesame oil; stir-fry until eggs are just cooked.

SERVES 4

Must be made just before serving

Above Singapore noodles
Opposite Chinese roast pork with stacked noodle omelettes

LAMB CUTLETS WITH THYME-TOASTED NOODLES

We used a locally made thin fresh Chinese egg noodle here which complemented the toasted breadcrumbs nicely.

1/3 cup (80ml) olive oil
4 cups (280g) stale breadcrumbs
2 cloves garlic, crushed
2 teaspoons chopped fresh thyme
12 (800g) lamb cutlets
150g button mushrooms,
  sliced thinly
1 cup (250ml) dry red wine
3/4 cup (180ml) water
3/4 cup (180ml) beef stock
1 1/2 tablespoons Dijon mustard
1 tablespoon tomato paste
420g fresh egg noodles

Heat 1/4 cup (60ml) of the oil in large pan; cook breadcrumbs, garlic and thyme, stirring, 15 minutes or until golden and crisp. Place breadcrumbs in large bowl.

Heat remaining oil in same pan; cook cutlets, in batches, until browned both sides and cooked as desired. Cover to keep warm. Add mushrooms to same pan; cook, stirring, until just soft. Add combined wine, water, stock, mustard and paste. Bring to boil; simmer, uncovered, about 10 minutes or until reduced by half, stirring occasionally.

Meanwhile, cook noodles in large pan of boiling water, uncovered, until just tender; drain. Gently toss noodles with toasted breadcrumbs in large bowl. Divide noodles among serving plates; top with cutlets; spoon sauce over top.

SERVES 4

Best made on day of serving

SLIP, SLOP, SLURP Throughout Asia, lusty slurping of noodles is regarded more as a compliment to the cook than bad manners. In Japan, for instance, participants in Zen retreats are only allowed to break their silence when they eat noodles as it is believed impossible to eat them quietly.

Opposite Lamb cutlets with thyme-toasted noodles
Above Satay beef noodles

SATAY BEEF NOODLES

Fresh chow mein are becoming easier to obtain, with large supermarket chains stocking them these days. Substitute Hokkien mee, however, if you can't find fresh chow mein.

2 tablespoons peanut oil
750g beef rump steak, sliced thinly
1 medium (150g) onion, sliced
1 clove garlic, crushed
$1/2$ cup (130g) smooth peanut butter
$1/4$ cup (60ml) sweet chilli sauce
$2/3$ cup (160ml) coconut milk
$3/4$ cup (180ml) chicken stock
2 tablespoons lime juice
1 teaspoon sugar
1 tablespoon chopped fresh
    coriander leaves
450g fresh chow mein
50g garlic chives, halved lengthways

Heat half the oil in wok or large pan; stir-fry beef, in batches, until browned and almost cooked. Cover to keep warm.

Heat remaining oil in same pan; stir-fry onion and garlic until onion is soft. Add peanut butter, sauce, milk, stock, juice, sugar and coriander; stir-fry until heated through.

Meanwhile, rinse chow mein in hot water to separate; drain.

Return beef and any juices to pan. Gently toss chives and noodles with beef; stir-fry until just heated through.

SERVES 4

Best made just before serving

ROAST CAPSICUMS FILLED WITH PORK AND VEAL

Many Chinese dried wheat noodles have various vegetables added to the dough before they are extruded — although it's the vegetable's colour that dominates, not the taste. We used spinach-flavoured thin wheat noodles here but you can substitute them with the colour of your choice.

150g dried wheat noodles
1 tablespoon olive oil
1 medium (150g) onion, chopped
2 cloves garlic, crushed
2 small fresh red chillies, seeded, chopped finely
500g pork and veal mince
425g can tomatoes
80g cherry tomatoes, quartered
50g baby English spinach leaves
1 tablespoon chopped fresh oregano
2 medium (400g) red capsicums
2 medium (400g) green capsicums
2 medium (400g) yellow capsicums

BEEF, RAMEN AND BOK CHOY STIR-FRY

Ramen can be dressed up in dishes like this so that it no longer resembles the 2-minute variety we all have in our kitchens.

2 tablespoons peanut oil
500g lean beef strips
1 large (300g) red onion, sliced
1 tablespoon grated fresh ginger
2 cloves garlic, crushed
1 large (350g) red capsicum, sliced
600g baby bok choy, trimmed, sliced
225g ramen
2 tablespoons oyster sauce
1 tablespoon sweet chilli sauce
1 tablespoon black bean sauce
1 tablespoon soy sauce
2 teaspoons rice vinegar

Heat oil in wok or large pan; stir-fry beef, in batches, until browned and cooked as desired. Add onion, ginger, garlic and capsicum to same pan; stir-fry 2 minutes or until onion is almost soft. Add bok choy; stir-fry 1 minute.

Meanwhile, cook noodles in large pan of boiling water, uncovered, until just tender; drain. Place in large bowl; separate noodles with fork.

Return beef to pan; gently toss with noodles and combined sauces and vinegar. Stir-fry 2 minutes or until heated through.

SERVES 6

Best made just before serving

Cook noodles in large pan of boiling water, uncovered, until just tender; drain.

Heat oil in large pan; cook onion, garlic and chilli, stirring, until onion is soft. Add mince; cook, stirring, until browned. Add undrained crushed tomatoes. Bring to boil; simmer 10 minutes or until mixture thickens slightly. Add cherry tomatoes and spinach; cook, stirring, until spinach is just wilted. Remove from heat; stir in oregano and noodles.

Cut off and reserve tops of capsicums; remove and discard seeds and membranes from all capsicums. Place capsicums in oiled baking dish; fill with noodle mixture, replace tops. Bake, uncovered, in moderate oven about 45 minutes or until capsicums are tender and browned lightly.

SERVES 4 TO 6

Can be prepared 3 hours ahead

Storage Covered, in refrigerator

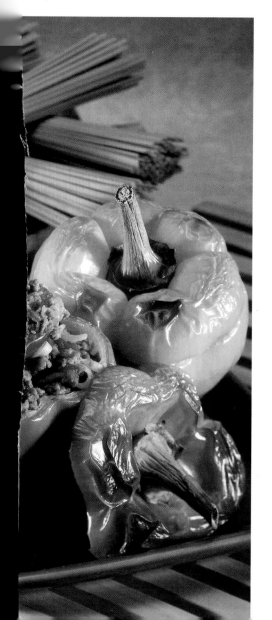

BEEF STROGANOFF WITH A TRIO OF MUSHROOMS

Triple the mushrooms and incorporate the noodles for this new-look stroganoff.

250g dried egg noodles
2 tablespoons olive oil
500g whole piece beef eye fillet, cut into thin strips
2 large (400g) onions, sliced
2 cloves garlic, crushed
150g oyster mushrooms, sliced
150g Swiss brown mushrooms, sliced
150g shimeji mushrooms, trimmed
1 tablespoon tomato paste
1 tablespoon Worcestershire sauce
2 teaspoons sweet paprika
1¹/₄ cups (300ml) sour cream
1 cup (250ml) beef stock
2 teaspoons lemon juice

Cook noodles in large pan of boiling water, uncovered, until just tender; drain. Rinse under cold water; drain.

Heat half of the oil in large pan; cook beef, in batches, until browned.

Heat remaining oil in same pan; cook onions and garlic, stirring, until onions are soft. Add mushrooms; cook, stirring, 2 minutes. Return beef to pan with combined paste, sauce, paprika, cream, stock and juice. Bring to boil; simmer 10 minutes. Gently toss noodles with beef mixture in pan until heated through.

SERVES 4 TO 6

Best made just before serving

Opposite Beef, ramen and bok choy stir-fry
Left Roast capsicums filled with pork and veal
Above Beef stroganoff with a trio of mushrooms

TERIYAKI BEEF WITH SOMEN

Any thin, round wheat noodle can be used
with teriyaki beef but somen makes
it more authentically Japanese.

1/4 cup (60ml) peanut oil
750g whole piece beef eye fillet,
   sliced thinly
1 large (200g) onion, sliced
2 cloves garlic, crushed
2 teaspoons grated fresh ginger
185g somen
1/4 cup (60ml) teriyaki sauce
1 tablespoon salt-reduced soy sauce
2 tablespoons mirin
6 green onions, chopped

Heat 2 tablespoons of the oil in wok or
large pan; stir-fry beef, in batches, until
browned. Heat remaining oil in same pan;
stir-fry onion, garlic and ginger 2 minutes.

Meanwhile, cook noodles in large pan
of boiling water, uncovered, 1 minute
only; drain. Rinse under cold water; drain.

Add combined sauces and mirin with
green onion; stir-fry until mixture is
heated through. Return beef to pan with
noodles; stir-fry 2 minutes or until
noodles are heated through.

SERVES 4

Best made just before serving

VEAL AND GREEN BEAN MADRAS

We used veal shoulder, trimmed of all fat,
in this recipe. We used dried wide flat
wheat noodles from Taiwan which can be
hard to find, but any dried flat wheat
noodle will suit just fine.

2 tablespoons peanut oil
600g diced veal shoulder
1 medium (150g) onion, chopped
2 cloves garlic, crushed
2 tablespoons finely chopped
   fresh lemon grass
2 tablespoons finely chopped
   fresh ginger
1 teaspoon Madras curry powder
1 teaspoon ground turmeric
1 cup (250ml) beef stock
1 cup (250ml) coconut milk
1 teaspoon brown sugar
150g green beans, sliced
170g dried wheat noodles

Heat oil in large pan; cook veal, in
batches, until browned. Add onion,
garlic, lemon grass, ginger, curry powder
and turmeric to same pan; cook, stirring,
until onion is soft. Return veal to pan
with combined stock, milk and sugar.
Bring to boil; simmer, covered, 1 hour or
until veal is tender. Add beans; simmer,
uncovered, until beans are tender.

Just before serving, cook noodles in
large pan of boiling water, uncovered,
until just tender; drain. Stir noodles
gently into veal mixture.

SERVES 4

Best made just before serving

◻ **SOMEN** This extremely thin wheat
noodle from Japan is labelled somen
if it is eggless, tamago somen if it
contains egg. Usually sold dried in
bundles held together by a paper band,
somen makes a refreshing summer dish
when served chilled with ice cubes. Take
extreme care not to overcook somen as it
can quickly become gluggy.

Opposite Teriyaki beef with somen
Below Veal and green bean madras

SWEET-SOUR BEEF IN NOODLE BASKETS

It's important to use fresh noodles for this recipe so that you have the flexibility required to shape the baskets. To make the noodle baskets you will need to use 2 wire strainers, the kind available from kitchenware stores, make sure they are completely made of metal... handles and all.

500g whole piece beef eye fillet
1 tablespoon plum sauce
1 teaspoon balsamic vinegar
2 tablespoons cracked black pepper
150g cherry tomatoes, halved
2 teaspoons olive oil
1 medium (160g) yellow zucchini, sliced
1 medium (120g) eggplant, sliced lengthways
60g rocket, trimmed

GARLIC DRESSING
2 tablespoons olive oil
2 tablespoons balsamic vinegar
1 clove garlic, crushed

NOODLE BASKETS
180g fresh egg noodles
vegetable oil, for deep-frying

Brush beef with combined sauce, vinegar and pepper. Cover; refrigerate 3 hours or overnight. Place beef on rack in baking dish. Toss tomatoes with oil in small bowl; place on rack with beef. Bake, uncovered, in moderate oven 30 minutes or until beef is cooked as desired. Remove beef, cover; stand 10 minutes. Slice beef thinly; cover to keep warm.

Cook zucchini and eggplant on heated oiled griddle (or grill or barbecue) until browned and just tender. Tear half the rocket into pieces. Gently toss beef, tomatoes, zucchini, eggplant, torn rocket and half the Garlic Dressing in large bowl.

Divide remaining rocket among serving plates, place Noodle Baskets on rocket. Divide beef mixture among Noodle Baskets, drizzle with remaining Garlic Dressing.

Garlic Dressing Combine all ingredients in jar; shake well.

Noodle Baskets Divide noodles into 6 portions. Brush inside of 13cm wire strainer with oil; line with 1 portion of the noodles. Oil underside of 10cm strainer; press smaller strainer down firmly onto noodles. Heat oil in large pan; holding both handles together with an oven mitt, gently lower strainer baskets into hot oil. Deep-fry until noodles are golden brown and crisp; drain on absorbent paper. Repeat with remaining noodles.

SERVES 6

Noodle baskets can be made 1 day ahead

Storage In airtight container

Above Sweet-sour beef in noodle baskets
Opposite above Hokkien mee
Below Orange ginger lamb with crispy noodle triangles

HOKKIEN MEE

There are probably as many versions of Hokkien mee as there are of spaghetti bolognese, but they agree on one thing: the noodle variety. Thankfully, Hokkien mee are now easily located in the refrigerated section of almost every supermarket.

600g Hokkien mee
2 eggs, beaten
1 tablespoon water
1/4 cup (60ml) vegetable oil
2 tablespoons grated fresh ginger
4 cloves garlic, crushed
4 small fresh red chillies,
**   seeded, chopped**
2 teaspoons sugar
1 large (200g) red capsicum,
**   seeded, sliced**
1 small (150g) green capsicum,
**   seeded, sliced**
4 green onions, sliced
2 cups (100g) shredded
**   Chinese cabbage**
400g Chinese barbecue pork, sliced
1/3 cup (80ml) ketjap manis
1/4 cup (60ml) oyster sauce

Rinse noodles under hot water; drain. Transfer to large bowl; separate noodles with a fork.

Heat large oiled non-stick pan; pour in half the combined eggs and water. Swirl pan to make a thin omelette; cook until just set. Transfer omelette to board, roll tightly; cut into thin strips. Repeat with remaining egg mixture.

Heat 1 tablespoon of the oil in wok or large pan; stir-fry ginger, garlic, chilli and sugar until fragrant. Add vegetables; stir-fry until cabbage is just wilted. Remove vegetables from pan. Heat remaining oil in same pan; stir-fry noodles 2 minutes. Add vegetables, pork and combined sauces; stir-fry until heated through. Serve sprinkled with omelette strips.

SERVES 4 TO 6

Best made just before serving

ORANGE GINGER LAMB WITH CRISPY NOODLE TRIANGLES

This noodle version of rosti is great to serve with many dishes as a crunchy surprise — even the kids will love them.

1/2 cup (125ml) orange juice
2 teaspoons grated fresh ginger
2 cloves garlic, crushed
1 tablespoon thick teriyaki sauce
1 tablespoon sweet chilli sauce
2 tablespoons honey
12 (800g) lamb cutlets

CRISPY NOODLE TRIANGLES
375g fresh egg noodles
1/4 cup (60ml) peanut oil

Combine juice, ginger, garlic, sauces and honey in large bowl; add cutlets, turn to coat in marinade. Cover; refrigerate 3 hours or overnight.

Drain cutlets; reserve marinade in same bowl. Cook cutlets, in batches, in large heated oiled pan until browned both sides and cooked as desired, brushing with reserved marinade. Serve cutlets on Crispy Noodle Triangles.

Crispy Noodle Triangles Cook noodles in large pan of boiling water, uncovered, until just tender; drain. When cool, press noodles into 19cm x 29cm slab pan; refrigerate, 3 hours or overnight.

Turn noodle cake onto board; cut noodle cake in half lengthways. Cut each half into 3 pieces widthways; cut each piece diagonally in half to give 12 triangles. Heat oil in large pan; cook triangles, in batches, until browned and crisp. Drain triangles on absorbent paper.

SERVES 4

Lamb and noodle triangles can be prepared 1 day ahead

Storage Covered, separately, in refrigerator

MEE GORENG

A much-loved dish that translates simply as fried noodles, this is one of our favourite versions, in which we used Peking noodles.

500g fresh wheat noodles
vegetable oil, for deep-frying
1 small (80g) onion, sliced
2 tablespoons raw peanuts
2 tablespoons peanut oil
500g pork fillets, sliced thinly
5 cloves garlic, crushed
2 tablespoons grated fresh ginger
3 small fresh red chillies,
  seeded, chopped
10 fresh water chestnuts, sliced
18 snake beans, sliced
2 celery sticks, chopped
2 baby bok choy, chopped
2 green onions, chopped
1/3 cup (80ml) ketjap manis
2 tablespoons sweet chilli sauce
1 tablespoon tamarind concentrate
1/3 cup (80ml) vegetable stock
1 teaspoon sesame oil

Cook noodles in large pan of boiling water, uncovered, until just tender; drain.

Heat vegetable oil in small pan; deep-fry onion until browned. Drain onion on absorbent paper. Deep-fry peanuts in same hot oil until browned lightly. Drain on absorbent paper. Blend or process onion and peanuts until chopped finely.

Heat half the peanut oil in wok or large pan; stir-fry pork until browned both sides and cooked as desired. Remove pork; cover to keep warm. Heat remaining peanut oil in same pan; stir-fry garlic, ginger and chilli until fragrant. Add water chestnuts and vegetables; stir-fry 2 minutes. Return pork to pan with noodles, sauces, tamarind, stock and sesame oil; stir-fry until heated through. Serve sprinkled with deep-fried onion and peanut mixture.

SERVES 4

Best made just before serving

Opposite Mee goreng
Right Crusty lamb cutlets with coriander pesto

⊏ CRISPY NOODLES Many varieties of clear noodle — dried rice, bean thread, arrowroot, shirataki, harusame — will puff up into white fluffy shreds when deep-fried in hot oil. They can then be used as a garnish, a bed for other food to be served on or an ingredient, as in the Thai dish, mee krob. Pre-boiled fresh and dried egg noodles can also be deep-fried to make serving nests or edible bowls.

CRUSTY LAMB CUTLETS WITH CORIANDER PESTO

Thin rice stick noodles, when used, crushed, as a coating for cutlets, add spectacular crunch to this dish.

2 cups firmly packed fresh
  coriander leaves
1/4 cup (20g) grated romano cheese
2 tablespoons pine nuts, toasted
1 tablespoon balsamic vinegar
1/2 cup (125ml) olive oil
1 clove garlic, chopped
12 (800g) lamb cutlets
300g dried rice noodles
plain flour
2 eggs, beaten
vegetable oil, for deep-frying

Blend or process coriander, cheese, nuts, vinegar, olive oil and garlic until pureed. Combine cutlets and 1/4 cup of the coriander pesto in large bowl. Cover; refrigerate 3 hours or overnight.

Place remaining coriander pesto in small bowl; cover surface with plastic wrap, refrigerate until ready to use.

Bake cutlets in oiled baking dish, in hot oven, 10 minutes; cool 5 minutes.

Place noodles in plastic bag; crush into small pieces.

Toss cutlets in flour, dip in eggs; press into crushed noodles. Heat vegetable oil in large pan; deep-fry cutlets, in batches, until noodles are golden brown and puffed. Drain on absorbent paper. Stir remaining coriander pesto in small pan over heat until warm; serve with cutlets.

SERVES 4 TO 6

Marinated lamb and coriander pesto can be made 1 day ahead

Storage Covered, separately, in refrigerator

BAKED BEEF 'N' NOODLES

This is one the whole family will love, the tasty combination of beef with plump, flavoursome noodles will win you points every time.

500g Hokkien mee
2 tablespoons olive oil
1kg beef chuck steak, cut
  into 3cm cubes
1 large (200g) onion, sliced
4 cloves garlic, crushed
2 celery sticks, sliced
2 medium (240g) carrots, chopped
2 (120g) baby eggplants, sliced
¼ cup (60ml) dry red wine
1½ cups (375ml) beef stock
2 tablespoons tomato paste
415g can tomato puree
1 cup (70g) stale breadcrumbs
1½ cups (185g) grated
  cheddar cheese
1 tablespoon chopped fresh parsley

Rinse noodles in hot water; drain. Transfer to large bowl; separate noodles with a fork.

Heat half the oil in large pan; cook beef, in batches, until browned. Heat remaining oil in same pan; cook onion and garlic, stirring, until onion is soft. Add celery, carrots and eggplants; cook, stirring 5 minutes or until vegetables are just tender. Return beef to pan with wine, stock, paste and puree. Bring to boil; simmer, covered, about 1 hour or until beef is tender. Stir noodles gently into beef mixture.

Transfer beef and noodle mixture to 2.5-litre (10-cup) ovenproof dish; sprinkle with combined remaining ingredients. Bake, uncovered, in moderate oven about 25 minutes or until browned.

SERVES 4 TO 6

Can be prepared 1 day ahead

Storage Covered, in refrigerator

◧ **FRESH WHEAT NOODLES** Commonly labelled Hokkien mee or stir-fry noodles, these round, thick, yellow-beige noodles are the base for many stir-fried dishes. They do not usually contain egg, though some cookbooks suggest they do. The noodles separate readily if they are rinsed in hot water before adding to the recipe.

Opposite Baked beef 'n' noodles
Right Lamb shanks with baked noodles

LAMB SHANKS WITH BAKED NOODLES

We used fresh Peking noodles made from wheat flour but any fresh stir-fry noodle can be used instead.

2 tablespoons olive oil
8 (1.8kg) lamb shanks
1 medium (150g) onion, sliced
2 cloves garlic, crushed
2 x 400g cans tomatoes
¼ cup (60ml) dry red wine
¼ cup (60ml) tomato paste
1 cup (250ml) beef stock
4 sprigs fresh oregano
150g button mushrooms, halved
300g fresh wheat noodles

Heat oil in large flameproof dish; cook lamb, in batches, until browned all over. Cover lamb; reserve 1 tablespoon of dish juices, discard remainder.

Add onion and garlic to same dish; cook, stirring, until onion is soft. Return lamb to same dish with undrained crushed tomatoes, wine, paste, stock and oregano. Bake, uncovered, in moderate oven 1½ hours. Remove lamb from dish; gently stir mushrooms and noodles into juices in dish. Return lamb to dish; gently mix in among noodles. Bake, uncovered, about 25 minutes or until top is crisp.

SERVES 4 TO 6

Can be made 3 hours ahead

Storage Covered, in refrigerator

STIR-FRIED UDON AND CRISPY LAMB

Here is an unusual treatment of classic Japanese udon that is sure to impress. Substitute any dried flat wheat noodle, if you wish.

1 clove garlic, crushed
1/2 cup (125ml) hoisin sauce
1 tablespoon soy sauce
1 tablespoon sweet chilli sauce
1 tablespoon oyster sauce
750g whole piece lamb eye of loin, cut into thin strips
plain flour
vegetable oil, for deep-frying
350g udon
2 tablespoons water
500g choy sum

Combine garlic and sauces in large bowl; reserve 2 tablespoons of marinade mixture in jar, refrigerate. Add lamb to bowl; coat with remaining marinade. Cover; refrigerate 3 hours or overnight.

Drain lamb; discard marinade. Toss lamb in flour; shake off excess. Heat oil in large pan; deep-fry lamb, in batches, until browned and crisp. Drain on absorbent paper. Cover to keep warm.

Cook noodles in large pan of boiling water, uncovered, until just tender; drain.

Boil combined reserved marinade and water in wok or large pan; stir-fry choy sum until just wilted. Remove choy sum mixture; cover to keep warm. Add noodles to pan; stir-fry until heated through. Divide noodles among serving plates; top with choy sum then crispy lamb.

SERVES 4

Lamb can be prepared 1 day ahead

Storage Covered, in refrigerator

Above Stir-fried udon and crispy lamb
Opposite Curried beef and lime noodles

CURRIED BEEF AND LIME NOODLES

We used dried wide rice stick noodles here; an interesting alternative would be to use mung bean thread noodles. You need fine slices of capsicums and green onions to make curls.

1 small (150g) red capsicum
1 small (150g) yellow capsicum
4 green onions
250g dried wide rice noodles
1 tablespoon peanut oil
750g minced beef
1 medium (150g) onion, chopped
2 cloves garlic, crushed
2 kaffir lime leaves, torn
1/3 cup (80ml) red curry paste
2 teaspoons brown miso
2 tablespoons lime juice
2 tablespoons fish sauce
1 1/2 cups (375ml) beef stock
2 teaspoons cornflour
2 tablespoons fresh coriander leaves

Quarter capsicums; remove seeds. Place capsicum, skin-side down, on cutting board. Cut capsicum horizontally, removing membranes and some of the flesh until 2mm thick; discard membranes and flesh. Slice capsicum into 2mm strips.

Halve green onions lengthways; slice halves into 2mm-thick strips. Place capsicum and onion in large bowl of iced water. Cover; refrigerate 1 hour or until strips curl.

Place noodles in large heatproof bowl, cover with boiling water, stand only until just tender; drain. Rinse well under cold water; drain.

Heat half the oil in wok or large pan; cook beef, in batches, until well browned. Cover to keep warm.

Heat remaining oil in same pan; stir-fry onion, garlic and lime leaves until onion is soft. Add combined paste, miso, juice and sauce; stir-fry 1 minute. Add blended stock and cornflour. Bring to boil; simmer, stirring, until thickened slightly. Return beef to pan with noodles; stir-fry until heated through. Serve topped with drained curled capsicum and green onion strips, and coriander leaves.

SERVES 4 TO 6

Best made just before serving

◻ **UDON** Available fresh and dried, these Japanese broad white wheat noodles are similar to those found in chicken noodle soup. Particularly popular in southern Japan, udon built its reputation as a soup noodle, but is equally at home in stir-fries and hotpots.

Counting your chickens

■ If there is a cooking equivalent of the meeting of like minds, it's the combination of chicken and noodles. Both ingredients bring an amazing versatility to the partnership: they absorb flavours brilliantly, lend themselves to a host of preparation techniques and can be teamed with an enormous array of vegetables, herbs and spices. This gathering of recipes celebrates a marriage made in culinary heaven.

CHILLED SOBA WITH FENNEL AND CHICKEN

The global village comes alive in this dish, where East meets West in a lavishly presented cold main course.

250g soba
5 green onions
1/3 cup (80ml) chicken stock
1/3 cup (80ml) dry white wine
5cm piece fresh ginger, sliced
4 (680g) chicken breast fillets
1 medium (500g) bulb fennel, sliced thinly
1 tablespoon sesame seeds, toasted
1 tablespoon mirin
2 tablespoons seasoned rice vinegar
2 tablespoons light soy sauce
2 tablespoons peanut oil
1 tablespoon lemon juice
1/2 teaspoon sesame oil

Cook noodles in large pan of boiling water, uncovered, until just tender; drain. Cover; refrigerate 3 hours or overnight.

Chop white parts of onions; reserve green leaves. Combine white parts of onions, stock, wine and ginger in large pan. Bring to boil; simmer. Add chicken; poach, covered, about 10 minutes or until tender. Remove chicken; cut into 1cm slices. Strain stock mixture into large bowl, discard ginger and onion; return stock to same pan. Add fennel, bring to boil; simmer, stirring, until fennel is soft. Remove fennel; discard stock.

Thinly slice reserved green onion leaves. Gently toss with noodles, chicken, fennel and sesame seeds in large bowl with combined remaining ingredients.

SERVES 4 TO 6

Noodles and chicken can be prepared 1 day ahead

Storage Covered, separately, in refrigerator

LIME-ROASTED SPATCHCOCK WITH NOODLES

The combination of mint, lime and cucumber makes a real treat for summertime feasting. We used wide rice stick noodles to complement the lightness of this recipe.

2 x 500g spatchcock
4 cloves garlic, crushed
2 teaspoons ground ginger
2 tablespoons finely grated lime rind
200g dried rice noodles
20g butter, melted
2 (800g) telegraph cucumbers
1 teaspoon cumin seeds, toasted, crushed
1 teaspoon yellow mustard seeds, toasted, crushed
1/2 teaspoon ground coriander
2 teaspoons sugar
2 tablespoons chopped fresh mint leaves
1/2 cup (125ml) lime juice
1/3 cup (80ml) sweet chilli sauce
1 tablespoon finely chopped fresh lemon grass
1/4 cup (40g) pine nuts, toasted

Cut along both sides of spatchcock backbones; discard backbones. Cut in half between breasts. Rinse under cold water; pat dry. Place spatchcock halves, skin-side up, in oiled shallow baking dish. Combine garlic, ginger and rind in small bowl; press onto spatchcock. Cover; refrigerate 1 hour.

Place noodles in large heatproof bowl, cover with boiling water, stand until just tender; drain.

Brush spatchcock with butter; bake, uncovered, in hot oven about 30 minutes or until cooked.

Meanwhile, cut cucumbers in half widthways; using a vegetable peeler, cut cucumber into ribbons. Combine cucumber ribbons and noodles in large bowl with seeds, coriander, sugar and mint.

Combine juice, sauce and lemon grass in jar; shake dressing well.

Divide noodle mixture among serving plates; top with spatchcock, drizzle with dressing, scatter with pine nuts.

SERVES 4

Spatchcock and dressing can be prepared 1 day ahead

Storage Covered, separately, in refrigerator

COMBINATION CHOW MEIN

Everyone's favourite in a Chinese restaurant is easily replicated at home with this simple recipe.

vegetable oil, for deep-frying
200g dried chow mein
600g medium uncooked prawns
2 tablespoons peanut oil
3 (500g) chicken breast fillets,
  sliced into 1cm pieces
2 cloves garlic, crushed
1 tablespoon grated fresh ginger
1 large (350g) red capsicum, sliced
230g can water chestnuts,
  drained, sliced
6 green onions, sliced finely
250g Chinese cabbage, shredded
80g bean sprouts
1/3 cup chopped fresh garlic chives
1/4 cup (60ml) light soy sauce
1 tablespoon oyster sauce
1/2 teaspoon sesame oil
2 teaspoons cornflour
1/2 cup (125ml) chicken stock

Heat vegetable oil in large pan; deep-fry noodles, in batches, until puffed. Drain noodles on absorbent paper. Shell and devein prawns, leaving tails intact.

Heat half the peanut oil in wok or large pan; stir-fry chicken, in batches, until browned both sides and tender. Cover chicken to keep warm. Add prawns to same pan; stir-fry until prawns change colour. Remove prawns; cover.

Heat remaining peanut oil in same pan; stir-fry garlic, ginger, capsicum, water chestnuts and all but 1 tablespoon of the onions until capsicum is just tender.

Return chicken and prawns to pan; add cabbage, sprouts and chives, stir-fry until cabbage is just wilted. Stir in combined sauces, sesame oil and blended cornflour and stock; stir-fry until mixture boils and thickens. Serve with deep-fried noodles; sprinkle with remaining onions.

SERVES 4 TO 6

Must be made just before serving

Opposite Lime-roasted spatchcock
with noodles
Right Combination chow mein

CHICKEN FILLETS WITH SOBA AND ROCKET

The nutty flavour of these Japanese buckwheat noodles is enhanced by the piquancy of the peppercorns and rocket.

4 (680g) chicken breast fillets
2 medium (400g) red capsicums
250g soba
120g rocket, trimmed
1 medium (200g) red onion, sliced

GREEN PEPPERCORN DRESSING
3/4 cup (180ml) light olive oil
1/4 cup (60ml) white wine vinegar
1 tablespoon green
    peppercorns, drained
1 clove garlic, peeled
1 teaspoon sugar

Cook chicken on heated oiled griddle (or grill or barbecue), brushing with 1/4 cup (60ml) of the Green Peppercorn Dressing, until chicken is browned both sides and tender. Remove chicken; slice thinly.

Quarter capsicums, remove seeds and membranes. Roast under grill or in very hot oven, skin-side up, until skin blisters and blackens. Wrap capsicum pieces in plastic or paper, 5 minutes, peel away skin; cut capsicums into 8cm strips.

Cook noodles in large pan of boiling water, uncovered, until just tender; drain. Rinse under cold water; drain well.

Just before serving, gently toss chicken, capsicum and noodles in large bowl with torn rocket, red onion and remaining Green Peppercorn Dressing.

Green Peppercorn Dressing Blend or process all ingredients until smooth.

SERVES 4 TO 6

Best made just before serving

PENANG STIR-FRY NOODLES AND CARAMELISED CHICKEN

These spicy Asian flavours marry well with any fairly thin, dried wheat noodle.

400g dried wheat noodles
2 tablespoons vegetable oil
4 (680g) chicken breast fillets, sliced finely
5 cloves garlic, crushed
1 tablespoon finely chopped fresh ginger
2 tablespoons finely chopped fresh lemon grass
4 small fresh red chillies, seeded, chopped finely
1/3 cup (60g) palm sugar
2 tablespoons water
1/4 cup (60ml) oyster sauce
2 tablespoons fish sauce
2 teaspoons tamarind concentrate
1/4 cup (60ml) lime juice
1/4 cup fresh coriander leaves

Cook noodles in large pan of boiling water, uncovered, until just tender; drain. Heat half the oil in wok or large pan; stir-fry chicken, in batches, until browned and tender. Cover to keep warm. Add remaining oil to same pan; stir-fry garlic, ginger, lemon grass and chilli until fragrant. Stir in sugar and water; cook, stirring, until sugar caramelises. Return chicken to pan; stir-fry until coated in caramelised sugar mixture. Stir in noodles with combined sauces, tamarind and juice. Simmer until sauce thickens slightly. Just before serving, sprinkle with coriander leaves.

SERVES 4

Best made just before serving

◰ **DRIED WHEAT NOODLES** As the name suggests, these noodles are based on wheat flour. They may be coloured with dyes or vegetable extracts and come in various guises ranging from the flat ho fen to tangled cakes labelled mein or "instant" noodles. They are equally at home in soups or stir-fries, in which case they have to be pre-cooked before adding to the wok.

Left Penang stir-fry noodles and caramelised chicken
Opposite Chicken fillets with soba and rocket

RICE STICK-CRUSTED CHICKEN WITH GARLIC MASH

This crisp coating of whole dried rice stick noodles makes a great alternative to a traditional crumb coating.

100g dried rice noodles
4 (680) chicken breast fillets
plain flour
2 eggs, beaten
1 teaspoon hot paprika
1 teaspoon chicken stock powder
1 clove garlic, crushed
4 green onions, chopped finely
1/4 cup (60ml) olive oil
5 medium (1kg) potatoes, chopped
2 cloves garlic, crushed, extra
1/3 cup (25g) coarsely grated
    parmesan cheese
1/2 cup (125ml) buttermilk
1 tablespoon finely grated
    lemon rind
1 tablespoon chopped fresh parsley

Place noodles in large heatproof bowl, cover with boiling water, stand until just tender; drain.

Pound chicken fillets until of an even thickness. Toss chicken in flour, then dip in eggs; coat with combined noodles, paprika, stock powder, garlic and onions.

Heat oil in large pan; cook chicken until browned both sides and tender. Remove chicken; cover to keep warm.

Meanwhile, boil, steam or microwave potatoes until tender; drain. Mash potatoes in large bowl with the extra garlic, cheese and buttermilk.

Sprinkle chicken with combined lemon rind and parsley; serve with garlic mash.

SERVES 4

Best made just before serving

Below Rice stick-crusted chicken
with garlic mash
Right Massaman chicken curry
Opposite Chicken, pumpkin and kumara stew

MASSAMAN CHICKEN CURRY

We added dried wide wheat noodles to our recipe for this curry that originated in the kitchens of the Muslim traders in Thailand.

2 tablespoons peanut oil
9 (1kg) chicken thigh fillets, sliced
1 large (200g) onion, sliced
1 2/3 cups (400ml) coconut milk
250g dried wheat noodles
150g green beans, sliced

YELLOW CURRY PASTE
1 small (100g) red onion,
    chopped roughly
1 tablespoon roughly chopped
    fresh lemon grass
4 cloves garlic, chopped coarsely
3 small fresh red chillies, seeded,
    chopped coarsely
1 tablespoon roughly chopped
    fresh turmeric
1 tablespoon roughly chopped
    fresh ginger
2 teaspoons coriander seeds
3 fresh coriander roots,
    chopped coarsely

2 tablespoons fish sauce
3 kaffir lime leaves, torn
2 teaspoons sugar
2 tablespoons peanut oil

Heat oil in large pan; cook chicken, in batches, until browned. Cover to keep warm. Add onion to same pan; cook, stirring, until onion is soft. Add Yellow Curry Paste; cook, stirring, until fragrant. Return chicken to pan with milk; simmer, uncovered, 30 minutes.

Meanwhile, cook noodles in large pan of boiling water, uncovered, until just tender; drain.

Add beans to chicken curry in pan; cook, uncovered, until beans are just tender. Gently stir in noodles until just heated through.

Yellow Curry Paste Blend or process all ingredients until pureed.

SERVES 4

Massaman chicken curry best made close to serving. Yellow curry paste can be made 1 week ahead

Storage In airtight container, in refrigerator
Freeze Yellow curry paste suitable

CHICKEN, PUMPKIN AND KUMARA STEW

A fresh, quite wide egg noodle was our choice for this recipe, but any wheat noodle would suit, so long as it's fresh.

500g fresh egg noodles
4 (680g) chicken breast fillets
4 bacon rashers, chopped
700g butternut pumpkin, cut into 2cm pieces
1 tablespoon olive oil
1 small (80g) onion, chopped
2 small (500g) kumara, chopped
2 teaspoons chicken stock powder
2 1/2 cups (625ml) water
1/4 cup (60ml) cream
1 tablespoon fresh oregano

Place noodles in large heatproof bowl, cover with boiling water, stand until just tender; drain.

Cook chicken on heated oiled griddle (or grill or barbecue) until chicken is browned both sides and tender. Remove chicken; slice into 1cm pieces. Cover to keep warm.

Cook bacon on same griddle until crisp. Remove bacon; cover to keep warm.

Boil, steam or microwave pumpkin pieces until just tender; drain. Cover to keep warm.

Meanwhile, heat oil in large pan; cook onion, stirring, until soft. Add kumara and blended stock powder and water to pan; cook, uncovered, until tender. Blend or process kumara mixture until smooth; stir in cream.

Gently toss noodles and chicken with pumpkin, kumara mixture and two-thirds of the bacon in large bowl. Sprinkle with remaining bacon and oregano.

SERVES 6

Best made just before serving

CHICKEN FATTOUSH WITH SOBA

Good food crosses all borders. Here the classic Syrian-Lebanese fattoush combines with wholesome Japanese soba to result in a dish that will be loved universally.

4 (680g) chicken breast fillets
1 medium (170g) red onion
1 (400g) telegraph cucumber
150g pocket pitta bread
125g soba
250g cherry tomatoes, halved
1 large (350g) yellow capsicum, seeded, sliced
1/2 cup roughly chopped fresh flat-leaf parsley
1/4 cup roughly chopped fresh coriander leaves
2 tablespoons roughly chopped fresh mint leaves
1/2 cup (125ml) light olive oil
2 tablespoons lemon juice
2 teaspoons sumac
1 1/2 teaspoons ground cumin
1/4 teaspoon ground cinnamon
1 clove garlic, crushed
1/2 teaspoon sugar

Cook chicken on heated oiled griddle (or grill or barbecue) until browned both sides and tender. Remove chicken; slice into 1cm pieces. Halve onion, cut into 1cm wedges. Halve cucumber lengthways; discard seeds, slice diagonally.

Toast pocket pitta, uncovered, on oven rack in moderately hot oven for about 15 minutes or until brown and crisp; break into pieces.

Cook noodles in large pan of boiling water, uncovered, until just tender; drain. Rinse under cold water; drain.

Just before serving, gently toss chicken, onion, cucumber, pitta pieces and noodles in large bowl with the tomatoes, capsicum, herbs and combined remaining ingredients.

SERVES 6

Best made just before serving

CHICKEN, MUSHROOM AND VERMICELLI RISOTTO

The combination of risotto and mung bean thread noodles — most commonly referred to as vermicelli — gives an interesting twist to this Italian classic.

1.25 litres (5 cups) chicken stock
1 cup (250ml) dry white wine
¹/₄ cup (60ml) olive oil
4 (680g) chicken breast fillets
30g butter
4 cloves garlic, crushed
1 small (200g) leek, sliced
250g button mushrooms, sliced
50g shiitake mushrooms, sliced
50g oyster mushrooms, sliced
2 cups (400g) calrose rice
¹/₂ cup (40g) finely grated smoked
  cheddar cheese
2 tablespoons chopped fresh chives
1 tablespoon chopped fresh
  sage leaves
vegetable oil, for deep-frying
100g bean thread noodles

Add stock and wine to medium pan. Bring to boil; simmer, covered, until required.

Heat 1 tablespoon of the olive oil in large pan; cook chicken until browned both sides and tender. Remove chicken, cover; stand 5 minutes. Slice chicken into 2cm pieces; cover to keep warm.

Heat remaining olive oil and butter in same pan; cook garlic, leek and mushrooms, stirring, until mushrooms are soft. Add rice; cook, stirring, 2 minutes or until translucent. Stir in ¹/₂ cup (125ml) hot stock mixture; cook, stirring, about 3 minutes or until liquid is absorbed. Continue adding hot stock mixture, ¹/₂ cup (125ml) at a time; cook, about 3 minutes or until liquid is absorbed, stirring between additions. Total cooking time will be about 35 minutes or until rice is just tender. Stir in chicken, cheese, chives and sage; cover risotto to keep warm.

Heat vegetable oil in large pan; deep-fry noodles, in batches, until crisp. Drain noodles on absorbent paper.

Just before serving, stir noodles through risotto.

SERVES 4

Best made just before serving

◘ SOBA is made from buckwheat and varying proportions of wheat flour. A bowl of soba is the first meal of the year for many people in Japan, eaten at midnight to ensure good luck and health in the coming year. Hand-made soba is highly prized and soba masters are designated by the Japanese government with a hierarchy dictated by the number of years of experience. Only about one-tenth of the soba consumed is handmade, however, and in Australia, soba is generally only available dried.

Opposite Chicken fattoush with soba
Above Chicken, mushroom and vermicelli risotto

SESAME CHICKEN WITH MIXED GREEN VEGETABLES

We have used the crinkly noodle, originally from China, called ramen. Interestingly, they're the most popular noodle in Japan.

4 (680g) chicken breast
　fillets, sliced
1/4 cup (60ml) soy sauce
1/4 cup (60ml) plum sauce
1 tablespoon hoisin sauce
1/4 cup (60ml) honey
1/4 cup (60ml) dry sherry
250g ramen
300g green beans, sliced
150g snow peas
1 tablespoon peanut oil
2 tablespoons cornflour
4 green onions, chopped
160g bean sprouts
1 teaspoon sesame oil
1 tablespoon sesame seeds, toasted

Place chicken in large bowl; pour combined sauces, honey and sherry over chicken, stir until coated in marinade. Cover; refrigerate 3 hours or overnight.

Cook noodles in large pan of boiling water, uncovered, until just tender; drain. Rinse under cold water; drain.

Boil, steam or microwave beans and snow peas, separately, until just tender. Rinse under cold water; drain.

Drain chicken; reserve marinade. Heat peanut oil in wok or large pan; cook chicken, in batches, until browned both sides and tender. Add blended cornflour and reserved marinade to pan; stir until mixture boils and thickens. Return chicken to pan with noodles, beans, snow peas, onions, bean sprouts and sesame oil; stir-fry until just heated through. Just before serving, sprinkle with sesame seeds.

SERVES 4 TO 6

Best made just before serving

RED PESTO CHICKEN WITH NOODLES

As you can see from our photograph, we used green-coloured, spinach-flavoured noodles; a plain wheat noodle or another flavour would work just as well.

300g dried wheat noodles
1 tablespoon olive oil
6 (1kg) chicken breast fillets
1 medium (150g) onion, sliced
2 cloves garlic, crushed
1/4 cup (60ml) dry red wine
2 tablespoons chopped fresh basil leaves
1 cup (250ml) chicken stock
2/3 cup (190g) bottled pesto with basil and sun-dried capsicums
1/3 cup (25g) coarsely grated parmesan cheese
100g fetta cheese, crumbled

Cook noodles in large pan of boiling water, uncovered, until just tender; drain.

Heat oil in large pan; cook chicken, in batches, until browned both sides and tender. Cover; stand 5 minutes. Cut into 1cm slices; cover to keep warm.

Add onion and garlic to same pan; cook, stirring, until onion is soft. Stir in wine, basil, stock and pesto. Bring to boil; simmer about 5 minutes or until mixture thickens slightly. Add chicken and parmesan; stir until heated through.

Just before serving, gently toss noodles with chicken mixture, sprinkle with fetta.

SERVES 6

Best made just before serving

Opposite Sesame chicken with mixed green vegetables
Left Red pesto chicken with noodles

MEE KROB

This Thai crispy noodle dish with its sweet, sour and salty flavours has become a favourite in many of our homes. With the easy availability of these fine rice stick noodles, there is now no hassle reproducing this restaurant treat in your own kitchen.

vegetable oil, for deep-frying
125g dried rice noodles
1½ tablespoons peanut oil
2 eggs, beaten
1 tablespoon water
500g minced chicken
¼ cup (60ml) lemon juice
2 tablespoons fish sauce
2 tablespoons tomato sauce
1 teaspoon soy sauce
2 tablespoons brown sugar
2 teaspoons chopped fresh
red chillies
1 tablespoon chopped fresh
coriander leaves
3 green onions, sliced
300g firm tofu, chopped

Heat vegetable oil in large pan; deep-fry noodles, in batches, until puffed. Drain noodles on absorbent paper.

Heat 1 teaspoon of the peanut oil in wok or large pan; pour in half of the combined egg and water. Swirl heated pan to make a thin omelette; cook until just set. Transfer omelette to chopping board, roll tightly; cut into thin strips. Repeat with 1 more teaspoon of vegetable oil and remaining egg mixture.

Heat remaining oil in same pan; stir-fry chicken until browned and cooked through. Add combined juice, sauces, sugar, chilli and coriander; stir-fry 1 minute. Add onion, tofu and omelette strips; stir-fry until heated through. Just before serving, gently toss noodles through chicken mixture.

SERVES 4 TO 6

Best made just before serving

Below Mee krob
Opposite Chicken and noodles in radicchio bowls

CHICKEN AND NOODLES IN RADICCHIO BOWLS

Try a variety of combinations: use a crisp, green lettuce rather than radicchio; or vegetable-flavoured wide wheat noodles instead of plain ones.

2 tablespoons olive oil
3 (500g) chicken breast fillets
200g dried wheat noodles
250g tiny new potatoes, quartered
1 small (150g) red capsicum
1 small (150g) green capsicum
4 bacon rashers, chopped
125g button mushrooms, sliced
8 large radicchio leaves

BUTTERMILK DRESSING
½ cup (125ml) olive oil
1 tablespoon Dijon mustard
2 tablespoons red wine vinegar
1 teaspoon sugar
1 tablespoon chopped fresh basil
2 cloves garlic, crushed
½ cup (125ml) buttermilk

Heat half the oil in large pan; cook chicken, in batches, until browned both sides and tender. Cover chicken; stand 5 minutes. Cut into 1cm slices.

Cook noodles in large pan of boiling water, uncovered, until just tender; drain. Cover to keep warm.

Boil, steam or microwave potatoes until just tender; drain. Halve capsicums; remove and discard seeds and membranes, slice thinly.

Heat remaining oil in same pan; cook potatoes, stirring, until crisp and browned lightly. Remove from pan; cover to keep warm. Discard oil; add bacon to same pan; cook, stirring, until crisp. Drain on absorbent paper. Add capsicums and mushrooms to same pan; cook, stirring, until just soft.

Gently toss chicken and noodles in large bowl with potatoes, bacon and capsicum mixture. Just before serving, place 2 radicchio leaves on each of the 4 plates; divide chicken mixture among leaves, drizzle with Buttermilk Dressing.

Buttermilk Dressing Blend or process all ingredients until smooth.

SERVES 4

Best made just before serving

⊏ **DRIED RICE NOODLES** Called beehoon in China and sen mee in Thailand (sen means line, mee means thin), these fine noodles are the mainstay of a Malaysian laksa. Usually soaked in hot water for 5 minutes before use, except when making crispy noodle dishes such as mee krob where the step is unnecessary.

CRUNCHY NOODLE PIZZAS

Everyone knows Marco Polo took noodles from China to Italy but few would have guessed that they'd end up on a pizza.

1 tablespoon vegetable oil
8 (900g) chicken thigh fillets
2 x 26cm packaged pizza bases
200g fried noodles, crushed lightly
2 cups (200g) coarsely grated mozzarella cheese
1/2 cup (125ml) sweet chilli sauce
2 tablespoons soy sauce

PESTO
2 cups firmly packed fresh basil leaves
1/4 cup (35g) blanched almonds, toasted, chopped
2 cloves garlic, crushed
1/3 cup (80ml) olive oil

Heat oil in large pan; cook chicken, in batches, until browned both sides and tender. Drain chicken on absorbent paper; cut into 5mm slices.

Spread Pesto evenly over pizza bases; top with chicken. Sprinkle combined noodles and cheese over chicken; drizzle with combined sauces. Bake in moderate oven about 20 minutes or until pizza tops are browned and edges are crisp.

Pesto Blend or process all ingredients until smooth.

SERVES 6 TO 8

Best made just before serving

CHICKEN SPINACH LASAGNE

Fresh rice noodle sheets, on average, measure 40cm x 70cm when unfolded; there are usually 2 sheets to a 1kg package. They don't need pre-cooking for this recipe.

2 tablespoons olive oil
6 (1kg) chicken breast fillets
2 medium (300g) onions, sliced
2 cloves garlic, crushed
200g button mushrooms, sliced
1 bunch (500g) English spinach
100g butter
1/2 cup (75g) plain flour
2 1/2 cups (625ml) milk
1/4 cup (60ml) dry white wine
1 egg yolk
1/2 cup (40g) coarsely grated romano cheese
500g fresh rice noodle sheet

Heat half the oil in large pan; cook chicken, in batches, until browned both sides and tender. Cover; stand 5 minutes. Cut into 1cm slices.

Add onions and garlic to same pan; cook, stirring, until onions are soft. Remove from pan.

Heat remaining oil in same pan; cook mushrooms, stirring, until just soft. Drain on absorbent paper.

Boil steam or microwave spinach until wilted; rinse under cold water. Press out excess liquid; drain on absorbent paper.

Melt butter in medium pan; stir in flour until bubbling. Remove from the heat; gradually stir in milk then wine. Stir over heat until white sauce boils and thickens. Remove from heat; stir egg yolk and half the cheese into white sauce.

Cut noodle sheets into 9 pieces, each measuring 12cm x 16cm. Place 3 noodle pieces over base of oiled 2.5-litre (10-cup) ovenproof dish. Spread half the chicken, spinach, onion mixture and mushrooms over noodles; cover with 3 noodle pieces and half the white sauce. Repeat layering with remaining chicken, spinach, onion mixture and mushrooms, finishing with the last 3 noodle pieces. Pour remaining white sauce over noodles, sprinkle with remaining cheese.

Bake, uncovered, in moderate oven about 45 minutes or until top is browned.

SERVES 6

Can be made 1 day ahead

Storage Covered, in refrigerator

SPANISH CHILLI CHICKEN

Arroz con pollo, rice with chicken, is one of Spain's most famous dishes. Here, we swap the rice for dried wide egg noodles and find it's just as aromatically delicious.

- 1 tablespoon olive oil
- 9 (1.5kg) chicken thigh cutlets
- 2 (340g) chorizo sausages, sliced
- 1 large (300g) red onion, sliced
- 4 cloves garlic, crushed
- 2 teaspoons ground cumin
- 2 teaspoons sweet paprika
- 4 large (1kg) tomatoes, peeled, chopped
- 1 cup (250ml) chicken stock
- 2 tablespoons hot chilli sauce
- 2 tablespoons chopped fresh oregano
- 2 tablespoons lemon juice
- 250g dried egg noodles

Heat oil in large pan; cook chicken, in batches, until browned both sides and tender. Discard fat from chicken. Add chorizo to same pan; cook until browned. Add onion and garlic; cook, stirring until onion is soft. Add cumin and paprika; cook, stirring until fragrant. Stir in tomatoes, stock, sauce, oregano and juice. Return chicken to pan. Bring to boil; simmer, covered, about 30 minutes or until chicken is tender.

Meanwhile, cook noodles in large pan of boiling water, uncovered, until just tender; drain. Just before serving, gently toss noodles with chicken mixture.

SERVES 6 TO 8

Best made just before serving

◧ **BIRTHDAY NOODLES** In China, noodles are a symbol of longevity and are often served at birthday parties and as a "crossing the threshold to a new year" food. They are, of course, also eaten at weddings, funerals and just about any other occasion when hunger dictates the serving of food.

Opposite Crunchy noodle pizzas
Left Chicken spinach lasagne
Below Spanish chilli chicken

LARB-STYLE CHICKEN

Larb is a well-known Thai dish and its complex flavours combine to make a unique main course. We used chicken fillet rather than mince in our version.

- 4 (680g) chicken breast fillets
- 1 (400g) telegraph cucumber
- 250g asparagus, trimmed
- 150g dried rice noodles
- 3 green onions, sliced
- 1 medium (200g) red capsicum, seeded, sliced
- 80g bean sprouts
- 1/3 cup (50g) unsalted peanuts, toasted, chopped
- 1/4 cup chopped fresh mint leaves
- 2 tablespoons chopped fresh coriander leaves
- 1/3 cup (80ml) lime juice
- 1/4 cup (60ml) vegetable oil
- 2 tablespoons finely chopped fresh lemon grass
- 3 small fresh red chillies, seeded, finely sliced
- 1 1/2 tablespoons fish sauce
- 2 teaspoons brown sugar
- 1 clove garlic, crushed

Cook chicken on heated oiled griddle (or grill or barbecue) until browned both sides and tender. Remove from pan; cut into 1cm slices. Halve the cucumber lengthways; discard seeds, cut into 1cm slices. Cut asparagus into 3cm lengths; boil, steam or microwave until just tender. Rinse under cold water; drain.

Place noodles in large heatproof bowl, cover with boiling water, stand until just tender. Rinse under cold water; drain.

Combine chicken and noodles in large bowl with cucumber, asparagus, onion, capsicum, sprouts, half the peanuts and herbs. Just before serving, gently toss in combined remaining ingredients.

SERVES 6

Best made just before serving

Right Larb-style chicken
Opposite Char kway teow

CHAR KWAY TEOW

The classic Malaysian fried noodle dish travels easily to our kitchens now that fresh rice noodles are so easy to obtain. Make sure you purchase fresh noodles; otherwise they may break when you try to cut them.

1kg fresh rice noodle sheets
500g small uncooked prawns
1/4 cup (60ml) peanut oil
2 (340g) chicken breast
**   fillets, chopped**
4 small fresh red chillies,
**   seeded, chopped**
2 cloves garlic, crushed
2 teaspoons grated fresh ginger
2 eggs, beaten
5 green onions, sliced
160g bean sprouts
1 tablespoon light soy sauce
1 teaspoon thick soy sauce
1/4 cup (60ml) dark soy sauce
1/4 teaspoon sesame oil
1 teaspoon brown sugar

Cut noodle sheets into 2cm strips. Place noodles in large bowl, cover with warm water; gently separate noodles with hands. Stand noodles 1 minute; drain.

Shell and devein prawns, leaving tails intact; halve prawns crossways.

Heat 1 tablespoon of the peanut oil in wok or large pan; stir-fry chicken, chilli, garlic and ginger about 2 minutes or until chicken is tender. Remove from pan; cover.

Heat half the remaining peanut oil in same pan; stir-fry prawns about 2 minutes or until prawns change colour. Remove from pan; cover. Add eggs, onion and sprouts to same pan; stir-fry until egg is just set. Remove from pan; cover.

Add remaining peanut oil to same pan; stir-fry noodles and combined remaining ingredients 1 minute. Return chicken, prawns and egg mixture to pan; stir-fry until heated through.

SERVES 6

Best made just before serving

Fishing for compliments

■ If the noodle is a canvas, seafood is the ingredient that can elevate a simple dish to a work of art. We are twice-blessed when it comes to the fruits of the sea... we have a fabulous variety of fish and crustacea, and we are also fortunate to harvest them from some of the world's cleanest waters. This haul of recipes pays tribute to that bounty as it spans the menu from starters to main courses.

LIME AND WASABI SEAFOOD NOODLES

Use baby beetroot leaves for their colour, if available; however, baby English spinach leaves can be substituted with no loss of flavour. We used a yellow, vegetable-dyed, dried wheat noodle for its colour; experiment with the various different coloured wheat noodles just for the effect.

750g medium uncooked prawns
750g baby octopus
250g dried wheat noodles
250g scallops
100g baby beetroot leaves
1/2 cup (125ml) peanut oil
1 tablespoon cider vinegar
2 1/2 teaspoons wasabi
2 teaspoons finely grated lime rind
1 clove garlic, crushed

Shell and devein prawns, leaving tails intact. Discard heads and beaks from octopus; cut octopus in half.

Cook noodles in large pan of boiling water, uncovered, until just tender; drain. Cover to keep warm.

Cook seafood, in batches, on heated oiled griddle (or grill or barbecue) until just cooked.

Combine seafood and noodles in large bowl with beetroot leaves and combined remaining ingredients.

SERVES 4 TO 6

Best made just before serving

SOBA WITH PRAWN TEMPURA

Traditional tempura takes a Western turn with this chilled vegetable and soba dish.

Beautiful buckwheat soba is just one of several Japanese noodles we have adopted; watch out for them in all Asian food shops.

250g soba
1 medium (120g) carrot
4 green onions
1 medium (200g) red capsicum
1 medium (200g) yellow capsicum
1 medium (200g) green capsicum
1 tablespoon sesame seeds, toasted
1kg medium uncooked prawns
1 egg yolk
1¼ cups (310ml) iced water
1 cup (150g) plain flour
extra plain flour
vegetable oil, for deep-frying
2 sheets nori, cut into 5mm pieces

LEMON SOY DRESSING
½ cup (125ml) peanut oil
1 tablespoon soy sauce
1 tablespoon seasoned rice vinegar
1 teaspoon wasabi
½ teaspoon sesame oil
2 tablespoons lemon juice

Cook noodles in large pan of boiling water, uncovered, until just tender; drain. Rinse under cold water; drain.

Cut carrot and onions into very thin, 8cm-long strips. Halve capsicums; remove and discard seeds and membranes. Slice capsicum into very thin strips.

Gently toss noodles, carrot, onion and capsicum in large bowl with sesame seeds and Lemon Soy Dressing; refrigerate while making prawn tempura.

Shell and devein prawns, leaving tails intact. Cut prawns along back almost all the way through; flatten slightly.

Just before serving, combine egg yolk and water in medium bowl; stir in sifted flour all at once. Do not overmix; mixture should be lumpy. Toss prawns in extra flour, shake off excess.

Heat vegetable oil in large pan. Dip prawns, in batches, in batter; deep-fry until prawns are cooked and browned lightly. Drain on absorbent paper. Deep-fry nori in same hot oil until just crisp; drain on absorbent paper.

Divide cold soba mixture among serving plates; top with prawn tempura, sprinkle with nori.

Lemon Soy Dressing Place ingredients in medium bowl; whisk until well combined.

SERVES 6

Prawn tempura must be made just before serving. Soba can be prepared 3 hours ahead

Storage Covered, in refrigerator

Above Soba with prawn tempura
Opposite Baked trout with orange hazelnut glaze

BAKED TROUT WITH ORANGE HAZELNUT GLAZE

The subtle nature of this fish calls for an equally delicate noodle, so we used a vermicelli-like, extra-thin wheat noodle.

300g dried wheat noodles
20g butter
1 large (180g) carrot, sliced finely
1 medium (350g) leek, sliced finely
1 teaspoon finely grated orange rind
$2/3$ cup (80g) hazelnuts, toasted, chopped
4 rainbow trout
30g butter, extra
1 cup (250ml) orange juice

Cook noodles in large pan of boiling water, uncovered, until just tender; drain. Rinse under cold water; drain.

Melt butter in medium pan; cook carrot and leek, stirring, until soft. Stir in noodles, rind and half the nuts; divide noodle mixture in half.

Divide one of the halves of the noodle mixture equally among the cavities of each trout; place filled trout, in single layer, in oiled baking dish. Bake, uncovered, in moderate oven about 20 minutes or until cooked through.

Meanwhile, melt extra butter in small pan, add juice; simmer, uncovered, about 5 minutes or until mixture is reduced by a third. Stir remaining nuts into glaze.

Reheat remaining noodle mixture in medium pan. Serve trout over noodle mixture with glaze.

SERVES 4

Best made just before serving

◰ **SOBA** comes in varying proportions of buckwheat and wheat flour, usually between 20% to 40% buckwheat. The colour varies accordingly, from brownish through to almost white, with cha-soba, to which powdered tea is added, being quite green. There are many claims for soba's health benefits, so it is often served as a kind of digestive at the end of a multi-course meal.

MIXED SEAFOOD IN A PUMPKIN BASKET

We used a straight ramen variety here, but any dried wheat noodle can be pre-cooked just before being mixed into the filling.

4 large (1.8kg) golden nugget pumpkins
6 small black mussels
16 (400g) medium uncooked prawns
4 (200g) small squid hoods
1 teaspoon vegetable oil
4 cloves garlic, crushed
2 teaspoons grated fresh galangal
1 tablespoon chopped fresh lemon grass
1²/₃ cups (400ml) coconut cream
1 tablespoon fish sauce
2 tablespoons mild chilli sauce
¹/₃ cup firmly packed fresh coriander leaves
2 kaffir lime leaves, torn
20 (400g) large white scallops
150g ramen

Place whole pumpkins on oiled oven tray; bake, uncovered, in moderately hot oven about 45 minutes or until tender.

Meanwhile, scrub mussels and remove beards. Shell and devein prawns, leaving tails intact. Cut squid hoods in half; lightly score inside surface with a criss-cross pattern, cut into 3cm pieces.

Discard tops and seeds of pumpkins. Scoop out flesh to within 5mm of skin; reserve 1 cup pumpkin flesh, discard remainder. Cover pumpkin to keep warm.

Heat oil in medium pan; cook garlic, galangal and lemon grass, stirring, about 1 minute. Add cream, sauces, coriander and reserved pumpkin flesh. Blend or process coconut mixture until almost smooth. Return coconut mixture to same pan; bring to boil. Add lime leaves and all seafood; simmer, stirring occasionally, until seafood is just tender and changed in colour.

Just before serving, cook noodles in large pan of boiling water, uncovered, until just tender; drain. Gently toss noodles into seafood mixture in pan; divide mixture among pumpkins.

SERVES 4

Best made just before serving

CREAMY LIME NOODLES WITH SMOKED SALMON

A refined wheat noodle such as somen is a perfect choice for this light yet flavourful dish. Off-cuts of smoked salmon are both economic and well-suited to this recipe.

500g dried wheat noodles
1 tablespoon peanut oil
¹/₂ small (50g) red onion, chopped finely
2 small fresh red chillies, seeded, chopped
1 tablespoon finely grated lime rind
1 tablespoon lime juice
2¹/₃ cups (600ml) light (18% fat) cream
¹/₂ cup (75g) chopped macadamias, toasted
240g smoked salmon, chopped
120g rocket, trimmed

Cook noodles in large pan of boiling water, uncovered, until just tender; drain. Cover to keep warm.

Heat oil in wok or large pan; stir-fry onion, chilli and rind until onion is soft. Stir in juice, cream, nuts and salmon; simmer until sauce thickens slightly.

Just before serving, gently toss noodles and rocket in large bowl with salmon cream mixture.

SERVES 4 TO 6

Best made just before serving

CRAB, GOAT CHEESE AND CHIVE ROSTI

These exquisite patties, accompanied by a green salad, make a perfect light lunch. The thin fresh egg noodles we used complement the clean, mild flavour of the dish.

150g fresh egg noodles
6 eggs, beaten
1/2 cup (125ml) cream
1/4 cup (35g) plain flour
500g fresh crab meat, shredded
200g firm mild goat
**   cheese, crumbled**
1/4 cup chopped fresh chives

Cook noodles in large pan of boiling water, uncovered, until just tender; drain. Rinse under cold water; drain. Chop noodles coarsely.

Combine eggs and cream in large bowl; gradually stir in flour. Stir in noodles, crab, cheese and chives.

Coat 7.5cm egg rings with cooking oil spray; place in large heated oiled pan. Place 1/4 cup of rosti mixture into each ring; cook, on both sides, until browned and cooked through.

Repeat with remaining rosti mixture.

MAKES ABOUT 24

Best made just before serving

Opposite Mixed seafood in a pumpkin basket
Above Creamy lime noodles with smoked salmon
Right Crab, goat cheese and chive rosti

PHAD THAI

We used sen lek, the 5mm-wide rice stick noodle traditionally used in this Thai classic. You can substitute poultry, if you prefer, for the prawns and pork, or make a vegetarian pad Thai using deep-fried tofu.

375g dried rice noodles
1/4 cup (65g) palm sugar
2 teaspoons soy sauce
1 tablespoon tomato sauce
1/4 cup (60ml) mild chilli sauce
1/4 cup (60ml) fish sauce
1 tablespoon peanut oil
200g minced pork
2 cloves garlic, crushed
1 tablespoon grated fresh ginger
3 eggs, beaten
200g medium cooked prawns, shelled
2 teaspoons chopped fresh red chillies
2 green onions, sliced
160g bean sprouts

BARBECUED OCTOPUS WITH STRINGHOPPERS

The Sri Lankan stringhopper is an indigenous "noodle" to the subcontinent where, not unlike pappadums, it is more often purchased from specialist makers than prepared from scratch at home. Look for them in Indian and Sri Lankan food shops.

1kg baby octopus
1/4 cup (60ml) lemon juice
1 clove garlic, crushed
2 (800g) corn cobs
250g cherry tomatoes, halved
300g curly endive, chopped
2 tablespoons lemon juice, extra
1/4 cup (60ml) light olive oil
1 tablespoon sweet chilli sauce
1 tablespoon chopped fresh mint leaves
vegetable oil, for deep-frying
150g stringhoppers

Remove and discard heads and beaks from octopus; cut in half. Combine octopus with juice and garlic in large bowl. Cover; refrigerate 30 minutes.

Remove husks from corn. Boil, steam or microwave corn until just tender; drain. Chop corn into 4cm pieces; cut pieces into quarters.

Drain octopus; discard marinade. Cook octopus, in batches, on heated oiled griddle (or grill or barbecue) until just cooked. Cook tomatoes on same griddle until just softened.

Gently toss octopus, corn and tomatoes in large bowl with endive and combined extra juice, olive oil, sauce and mint in large bowl.

Heat vegetable oil in large pan; deep-fry stringhoppers until puffed. Drain on absorbent paper. Serve octopus mixture with stringhoppers.

SERVES 4 TO 6

Stringhoppers must be deep-fried just before serving. Octopus can be marinated 1 day ahead

Storage Covered, in refrigerator

**2 tablespoons chopped fresh
   coriander leaves**
**1/2 cup (75g) unsalted roasted
   peanuts, chopped**

Place noodles in large heatproof bowl,
cover with boiling water, stand until just
tender; drain. Cover to keep warm.

Combine sugar and sauces in small
pan; cook, stirring, until sugar dissolves.

Heat oil in wok or large pan; stir-fry
pork, garlic and ginger until pork is
browned and almost cooked. Add eggs
and prawns; cook, stirring gently, until
egg sets. Add noodles, sauce mixture and
remaining ingredients; gently stir-fry
until heated through. If desired, serve
with fresh lime wedges.

SERVES 4 TO 6

Best made just before serving

Left Barbecued octopus with stringhoppers
Below Phad Thai
Right South Indian grilled fish with
coconut masala

SOUTH INDIAN GRILLED FISH WITH COCONUT MASALA

While we used barramundi here, you can
substitute your favourite fish, cut into
steaks or cutlets, for this recipe. The fresh
wheat noodle pictured is lei mein, which
differs only from chow mein in that it is
slightly heavier and more dense.

**1/4 cup firmly packed fresh
   flat-leaf parsley**
**1/4 cup firmly packed fresh
   coriander leaves**
2 tablespoons lemon juice
2 tablespoons olive oil
1 tablespoon ground cumin
1 teaspoon ground coriander
1/2 teaspoon sweet paprika
1/4 teaspoon ground cinnamon
2 cloves garlic, chopped
**1 small fresh red chilli,
   seeded, chopped**
1/2 teaspoon salt
3/4 cup (90g) coconut milk powder
1 1/4 cups (310ml) boiling water
4 x 200g barramundi steaks
300g fresh wheat noodles

Blend or process fresh herbs, juice, oil,
ground spices, garlic, chilli and salt until
smooth. Place herb mixture in medium
pan with blended milk powder and water.
Bring to boil; simmer, stirring, 1 minute.

Cook fish on heated oiled griddle (or
grill or barbecue) until browned both
sides and cooked through.

Meanwhile, cook noodles in large pan
of boiling water, uncovered, until just
tender; drain.

Divide noodles among each of the
serving plates; top with fish, then heated
coconut masala.

SERVES 4

Best made just before serving

◻ **STRINGHOPPERS** are a Sri Lankan
specialty, made by forcing a rice-flour
batter through a perforated mould to
form a lacy circle about the size of a
saucer. Eaten as an accompaniment to a
rich main course, stringhoppers are tricky
to make but, fortunately, instant dried
versions are available at Asian food shops.

SICHUAN PRAWNS WITH NOODLE POLENTA BATONS

Fettuccine-like fresh egg noodles are chopped and mixed with polenta and pecorino to make crunchy batons that are a perfect foil for these spicy prawns.

20 (1kg) large uncooked prawns
2 tablespoons dry sherry
2 teaspoons sugar
1 tablespoon cider vinegar
200g fresh egg noodles
1 cup (250ml) vegetable stock
1/2 cup (125ml) water
1/2 cup (85g) polenta
1/2 teaspoon salt
1/4 cup grated pecorino cheese
1 tablespoon sesame oil
4 medium (200g) egg
    tomatoes, sliced
60g rocket, trimmed
2 tablespoons sweet chilli sauce
1 tablespoon dark soy sauce
1 tablespoon lime juice

Shell and devein prawns, leaving tails intact. Combine sherry, sugar, vinegar and prawns in medium bowl. Cover; refrigerate 1 hour.

Place noodles in medium heatproof bowl, cover with boiling water, stand until just tender; drain. Chop noodles coarsely.

Bring stock and water to boil in medium pan. Gradually stir in polenta and salt; cook, stirring, over low heat about 2 minutes or until mixture is thickened slightly. Stir in noodles and cheese. Pour into oiled deep 17cm-square cake pan. Cover; refrigerate until firm.

Just before serving, turn polenta onto board. Cut polenta in half; cut each half, crossways, into 8 x 2cm strips. Brush polenta batons with sesame oil; cook, in batches, on heated oiled griddle until golden brown both sides. Cover to keep warm. Cook prawns on same griddle until they change colour. Serve prawns with polenta batons, tomato and rocket; drizzle over combined remaining ingredients.

SERVES 4

*Polenta mixture can be prepared
1 day ahead*

Storage Covered, in refrigerator

Opposite Sichuan prawns with noodle polenta batons
Right Siberian salmon with soba blini

SIBERIAN SALMON WITH SOBA BLINI

It's perfectly natural to make blini with soba since these tiny Russian pancakes are traditionally made of buckwheat flour — the main ingredient in soba.

100g soba
6 eggs, beaten
^{2}/$_3$ cup (160ml) water
2 tablespoons fish sauce
1 tablespoon wasabi
1 sheet toasted nori, shredded
1^1/$_4$ cups (300ml) sour cream
1 tablespoon chopped fresh dill
1 small (100g) red onion, chopped
1 tablespoon olive oil
4 x 220g Atlantic salmon fillets
2 tablespoons lemon juice
2 tablespoons vodka
60g butter

Cook noodles in large pan of boiling water, uncovered, until just tender; drain. Rinse under cold water; drain. Cut into 2cm lengths.

Whisk eggs with water in large bowl until frothy; stir in sauce and wasabi.

Gently toss noodles and nori into egg mixture. Heat oiled 20cm crepe pan; add about ^{1}/$_3$ cup of egg mixture to pan, swirl to coat base. Cook until blini is set underneath then grill until top is just set; carefully slide blini onto board. Repeat with remaining egg mixture; you need 8 blini for this recipe.

Stack two blini; roll tightly in plastic wrap, secure ends. Repeat with remaining blini. Mix cream, dill and onion in small bowl; cover, refrigerate until required.

Just before serving, heat olive oil in large pan; cook salmon, in batches, until browned both sides and cooked as desired. Cover to keep warm. Add juice, vodka and butter to same pan; stir until butter melts.

Unwrap the blini parcels; cut each into 3 pieces. Divide blini pieces among serving plates with salmon, sour cream mixture and vodka butter sauce.

SERVES 4

Blini and sour cream mixture can be made 3 hours ahead

Storage Covered, separately, in refrigerator

POLENTA-PEPPERED TUNA WITH RICE NOODLE RIBBONS

For this recipe, we used 1 of the 2 fresh rice noodle sheets that are sold already packaged in 1kg bags, folded into pleats and sliced into 1.5cm ribbons.

4 x 2.5cm-thick tuna steaks
1/4 cup (40g) polenta
1 1/2 tablespoons coarsely ground black pepper
vegetable oil, for shallow-frying
500g fresh rice noodles, 1.5cm wide

BASIL DRESSING
1/3 cup (80ml) light olive oil
1/3 cup (80ml) olive oil
1/4 cup firmly packed fresh basil leaves
2 tablespoons lemon juice
1 tablespoon Dijon mustard
2 teaspoons honey

Brush tuna with water; coat in combined polenta and pepper. Heat oil in large pan; shallow-fry tuna, in batches, until browned both sides and cooked through.

Place noodles in large pan of boiling water, remove immediately; drain. Gently toss noodles in large bowl with a third of the Basil Dressing; divide noodles among serving plates. Top with tuna; drizzle with remaining dressing.

Basil Dressing Blend or process all ingredients until smooth.

SERVES 4

Best made just before serving

Below Polenta-peppered tuna with rice noodle ribbons
Right Coco-chilli prawns on a noodle nest

◖ **FRESH RICE NOODLE SHEETS** are a thoroughly versatile product, being used whole for lasagne-type dishes, cut into small rounds or squares for tortellini or ravioli, torn into fragments for "rag" pasta, or cut into long strips. To make noodles, gently unwrap the sheet, smoothing out any wrinkles. Fold sheet into thirds, then in half. Trim edges, then cut into the desired width.

COCO-CHILLI PRAWNS ON A NOODLE NEST

We used bundles of thin dried wheat noodles here, but any dried noodle — even bean thread — can be deep-fried for the desired effect of the prawns' nests.

30 (750g) medium
    uncooked prawns
1 tablespoon peanut oil
1 large (200g) onion, sliced
2 cloves garlic, crushed
2 teaspoons grated fresh ginger
1 tablespoon black mustard seeds
1 tablespoon ground cumin
1 tablespoon ground coriander
2 small fresh red chillies, seeded,
    chopped finely
4 fresh curry leaves, torn
1²/3 cups (400ml) coconut cream
1/2 cup (125ml) water
1 tablespoon chopped fresh
    coriander leaves
vegetable oil, for deep-frying
6 bunches (240g) dried
    wheat noodles

Shell and devein prawns, leaving tails intact. Heat peanut oil in large pan; cook onion, garlic and ginger, stirring, until onion is soft. Add seeds, cumin, coriander, chilli and curry leaves; cook, stirring, until seeds pop. Add combined cream and water. Bring to boil; simmer, uncovered, about 5 minutes or until sauce thickens. Add prawns; simmer, uncovered, about 5 minutes or until prawns change colour and are just cooked. Stir in coriander leaves.

Heat vegetable oil in large pan; deep-fry noodle bunches until puffed and browned lightly. Drain bunches on absorbent paper. Serve prawn mixture on noodle nests.

SERVES 4 TO 6

Best made just before serving

CAJUN-STYLE FISH WRAPPED IN BANANA LEAVES

We used ling here because it stands up to the cajun spices but you can use any firm white fish fillet when making this recipe.

4 large banana leaves
1 medium (400g) kumara, sliced thinly
1 teaspoon salt
1 teaspoon hot paprika
1 teaspoon cracked black pepper
1 teaspoon ground cumin
1 teaspoon ground oregano
4 x 250g boneless white fish fillets
375g fresh rice noodles
1 teaspoon peanut oil
2 teaspoons chopped fresh lemon grass
1 small fresh red chilli, seeded, chopped finely
1 cup (250ml) coconut cream
1 tablespoon chopped fresh coriander leaves
2 teaspoons lime juice

Cut each banana leaf into a 35cm square. Using tongs, submerge the squares, 1 leaf at a time, in large pan of boiling water; remove immediately. Rinse leaves under cold water; dry thoroughly. Leaves should be soft and pliable.

Boil, steam or microwave kumara until almost tender; drain.

Combine salt, paprika, pepper, cumin and oregano in medium bowl; coat fish fillets in spice mixture.

Place noodles in large heatproof bowl, cover with boiling water, stand until just tender; drain.

Divide noodles and kumara among banana leaves; top with fish fillets. Fold opposite sides of leaves over fish fillets; repeat with remaining sides.

Place parcels, seam-side down, in single layer, in oiled baking dish. Bake, uncovered, in moderate oven about 35 minutes or until fish is tender.

Meanwhile, heat oil in small pan; cook lemon grass and chilli, stirring, 1 minute. Stir in cream, coriander and juice. Bring to boil; simmer, uncovered, about 2 minutes or until sauce thickens slightly.

Place fish parcels, seam-side up, on serving plates; open out corners of banana leaves slightly, drizzle fish with warm coconut sauce.

SERVES 4

Best made just before serving

NOODLE AND PRAWN CHERMOULLA

Chermoulla is just one of the many Moroccan flavours that has crept into our kitchen today. Used as a marinade or sauce, like salsa or masala, it is made of herbs and spices according to the taste of the individual cook but almost always contains fresh coriander, cumin and paprika.

40 (1kg) medium uncooked prawns
150g dried rice noodles
2 tablespoons olive oil
5 medium (950g) tomatoes, peeled, seeded, sliced
1/4 cup roughly chopped fresh flat-leaf parsley

CHERMOULLA
1/3 cup firmly packed fresh coriander leaves
1/3 cup firmly packed fresh flat-leaf parsley
1/4 cup (60ml) olive oil
2 tablespoons lemon juice
2 small fresh red chillies, seeded, chopped
2 cloves garlic, chopped
2 teaspoons ground cumin
1 teaspoon sweet paprika
1 teaspoon ground coriander
1/2 teaspoon salt

Shell and devein prawns, leaving tails intact. Combine prawns with half the Chermoulla in medium bowl. Cover; refrigerate 3 hours or overnight.

Place noodles in medium heatproof bowl, cover with boiling water, stand only until just tender; drain.

Just before serving, heat oil in wok or large pan; stir-fry prawns until changed in colour and almost cooked. Add noodles; stir-fry until heated through. Remove from heat. Gently toss prawn mixture in large bowl with remaining Chermoulla, tomato and parsley.

Chermoulla Blend or process all ingredients until almost pureed.

SERVES 4

Prawns best marinated 1 day ahead

Storage Covered, in refrigerator

⊏ **IDENTITY CRISES** Many words — soba, udon, ramen, mee, kway teow, mein, bee hoon and sen, to name a few — either actually mean, or incorporate the sense of, "noodle" in their translations. Therefore, in recipes and on menus, it would be repetitive to follow the name with the word noodle. So when you see a dish called yum wun sen, zaru-soba, mee krob or char kway teow, you automatically know it's a noodle dish.

ORIENTAL CHILLI SQUID PACKAGES

We used mung bean thread noodles to help bind the squid filling, but a thin fresh rice noodle would work just as well.

14 Chinese dried mushrooms
250g bean thread noodles
1 tablespoon vegetable oil
4 cloves garlic, crushed
1 tablespoon chopped fresh lemon grass
230g can water chestnuts, drained, chopped
8 green onions, chopped
2 tablespoons chopped fresh mint leaves
200g shelled cooked prawns, chopped
1/4 cup (60ml) sweet chilli sauce
1/4 cup (60ml) sweet soy sauce
10 medium (850g) squid hoods
3 teaspoons salt
2 tablespoons sugar
1/3 cup (40g) mild chilli powder
2 tablespoons ground ginger
2 tablespoons vegetable oil, extra
1/3 cup chopped fresh coriander leaves
150g butter, melted

Place mushrooms in small heatproof bowl, cover with boiling water, stand about 20 minutes or until soft; drain. Discard stems; chop caps finely.

Place noodles in medium heatproof bowl, cover with boiling water, stand until just tender; drain. Cut noodles into 4cm lengths.

Heat oil in large pan; cook garlic, lemon grass and water chestnuts, stirring, until fragrant. Add mushrooms, noodles, onion, mint, prawns and sauces; stir until combined. Fill squid hoods with noodle mixture; secure openings with skewers. Combine salt, sugar, chilli powder and ginger in large plastic bag; shake filled squid in bag, 1 at a time, to coat in spice mixture.

Place squid in large oiled baking dish, in single layer; drizzle with extra oil. Bake, uncovered, in moderate oven about 40 minutes or until squid is tender. Serve with combined coriander and butter.

SERVES 4 TO 6

Filled squid best cooked just before serving but can be prepared up to 3 hours ahead

Storage Covered, in refrigerator

Opposite Cajun-style fish wrapped in banana leaves
Above Noodle and prawn chermoulla
Left Oriental chilli squid packages

FRESH SALMON, CAPER AND DILL FRITTATA

The wholesomeness of creamy-white udon is the perfect match for that delectable combination of salmon, dill, capers and cream. A thin fresh egg noodle can be substituted if you cannot find Japanese udon in your area. Start with salmon either in a single piece or as fillets because it's ultimately to be flaked in the frittata.

1 tablespoon olive oil
500g Atlantic salmon
1 medium (150g) onion, sliced
150g dried udon

6 eggs, beaten
3/4 cup (180ml) cream
1 tablespoon chopped fresh dill
1/4 cup (40g) capers, chopped
1/4 teaspoon cracked black pepper
3/4 cup (180ml) light sour cream
1 tablespoon drained green peppercorns, chopped

Oil a deep 28cm-round cake pan, line base with baking paper.

Heat oil in large pan; cook salmon until browned both sides and just cooked through. Remove from pan; break with fork into large flakes. Add onion to same pan; cook until soft.

Cook noodles in large pan of boiling water, uncovered, until just tender; drain. Rinse under cold water; drain.

Combine eggs with cream in large bowl; gently stir in salmon, onion, noodles, dill, capers and black pepper. Pour frittata mixture into prepared pan; bake, uncovered, in moderate oven about 30 minutes or until set. Stand frittata 5 minutes before turning out; serve with combined sour cream and peppercorns.

SERVES 4

Best made just before serving

SHANGHAIED PRAWNS AND STIR-FRIED VEGETABLES

We wrapped these prawns in fresh Shanghai noodles, made of wheat flour, which need no pre-cooking before being deep-fried around the seafood.

30 (750g) medium uncooked prawns
1 clove garlic, crushed
2 tablespoons lemon juice
2 tablespoons sweet chilli sauce
2 teaspoons soy sauce
1 tablespoon chopped fresh coriander leaves
200g fresh Shanghai noodles
3 medium (360g) carrots
3 medium (600g) red capsicums, seeded
3 green onions, trimmed
vegetable oil, for deep-frying
20g butter
1 tablespoon peanut oil
3 cloves garlic, crushed, extra
240g bean sprouts
1 teaspoon soy sauce, extra

Shell and devein prawns, leaving tails intact. Combine prawns with garlic, juice, sauces and coriander in medium bowl. Cover; refrigerate 3 hours or overnight.

Drain prawns; discard marinade.

Place noodles flat on tray to make them easier to work with. Pick up 2 noodles, loop them around prawn tail to secure; wrap noodles around prawn to cover. If first 2 noodles are not long enough to cover whole prawn, pick up 2 more, pressing their ends at loose ends of original 2 noodles to secure. Place wrapped prawns, noodle-end side down, in single layer on tray. Cover; refrigerate 30 minutes.

Cut carrots, capsicums and onions into long, thin strips.

Just before serving, heat vegetable oil in large pan; deep-fry prawns, in batches, until prawns are cooked through; drain on absorbent paper.

Heat butter and peanut oil in wok or large pan; stir-fry extra garlic, carrot, capsicum, onion, sprouts and extra sauce until vegetables are just tender. Serve prawns on bed of stir-fried vegetables.

SERVES 4 TO 6

Prawns best marinated 1 day ahead

Storage Covered, in refrigerator

Opposite Fresh salmon, caper and dill frittata
Right Shanghaied prawns and stir-fried vegetables

Ca'noodling with vegetables

 The profusion of exotic and exciting newcomers on the greengrocer's shelves has given us a new appreciation of vegetables. Toss with one of the startling variety of noodles now easily found at the supermarket, add a dash of inspiration from Asia and the Mediterranean, and you'll find there are whole new avenues to be explored. Creative cooks will reap rewards when they take a fresh look at the vegie patch.

GRILLED HALOUMI, TOMATO AND ROCKET HOKKIEN MEE

Very today, this amalgam of Mediterranean flavours is tossed in the melting pot with one of the best-loved of all Asian noodles.

14 large (1.3kg) egg tomatoes, halved lengthways
1 tablespoon olive oil
2 teaspoons balsamic vinegar
1/2 teaspoon salt
1 teaspoon cracked black pepper
1 bulb (45g) garlic, unpeeled
2 teaspoons balsamic vinegar, extra
1/2 cup (125ml) vegetable stock
600g Hokkien mee
400g haloumi cheese
240g rocket, trimmed

Place tomatoes, cut-side up, on wire rack over baking dish; drizzle with combined oil and vinegar, sprinkle with combined salt and pepper. Wrap garlic in foil; place on rack with tomatoes.

Bake tomatoes, uncovered, and garlic in moderate oven 1 hour. Cover tomatoes with foil, bake 30 minutes. When garlic is cool enough to handle, peel; reserve pulp.

Blend or process half the tomatoes with garlic pulp, extra vinegar and stock until pureed.

Meanwhile, rinse noodles under hot water; drain. Transfer to large bowl; separate noodles with fork. Cut haloumi into 1cm slices; cook on heated oiled griddle until browned lightly.

Just before serving, gently toss noodles in large bowl with pureed tomato mixture, remaining tomato halves, haloumi slices and torn rocket.

SERVES 4

Best made just before serving

EGGPLANT TIMBALES WITH ROASTED TOMATO SAUCE

Because of its supple texture once it's cooked, somen works particularly well as the major ingredient in the timbale filling. If you have to substitute it, use a similarly fine, dried thin wheat noodle.

1 large (500g) eggplant
coarse cooking salt
100g somen
1 tablespoon olive oil
1 medium (350g) leek, sliced thinly
1 medium (120g) carrot,
    grated coarsely
1 medium (120g) zucchini,
    grated coarsely

4 eggs, beaten
1 tablespoon chopped fresh oregano
1/4 cup (60ml) cream
1/2 cup (100g) crumbled
    fetta cheese
1/4 cup (20g) coarsely grated
    parmesan cheese

ROASTED TOMATO SAUCE
3 small (390g) tomatoes, halved
1 teaspoon salt
2 cloves garlic, crushed
1/4 cup (60ml) olive oil
1/2 teaspoon sugar
1 tablespoon red wine vinegar

Slice eggplant thinly, place on wire rack, sprinkle with salt; stand 30 minutes. Rinse under cold water; pat dry with absorbent paper. Cook eggplant on heated oiled griddle (or grill or barbecue) until browned lightly both sides.

Meanwhile, cook noodles in large pan of boiling water, uncovered, until just tender; drain. Heat oil in medium pan; cook leek, carrot and zucchini, stirring, until vegetables are soft. Transfer to large bowl; stir in noodles, eggs, oregano, cream and cheeses.

Overlap 4 eggplant slices over base and side of each of 4 x 1 1/4-cup (310ml) ovenproof dishes, extending eggplant slices slightly above edge of dishes. Divide noodle mixture among prepared dishes; fold eggplant over filling. Top timbales with remaining eggplant slices, pressing down firmly.

Cover timbales with foil, place on oven tray; bake in moderate oven about 35 minutes or until firm. Serve timbales with Roasted Tomato Sauce.

Roasted Tomato Sauce Place tomatoes in baking dish, sprinkle with salt and combined garlic and 1 tablespoon of the oil. Bake, uncovered, in hot oven about 20 minutes or until soft; cool. Blend or process tomatoes, remaining oil, sugar and vinegar until pureed. Press through fine sieve into small pan, discard skins; stir over medium heat until heated through.

SERVES 4

Eggplant timbales best made just before serving. Roasted tomato sauce can be made 1 day ahead

Storage Covered, in refrigerator

Opposite Eggplant timbales with roasted tomato sauce
Above Mixed-mushroom ragout with baked ricotta

MIXED-MUSHROOM RAGOUT WITH BAKED RICOTTA

Chinese wheat noodles which have had a small amount of dehydrated egg powder used in their manufacture add just the right amount of colour to this delicate recipe.

400g ricotta cheese
2 egg yolks
3 cloves garlic, crushed
$1/4$ cup chopped fresh chives
$1/4$ cup (60ml) dry white wine
30g butter
200g Swiss brown mushrooms, sliced finely
150g oyster mushrooms, sliced finely
100g enoki mushrooms
180g dried yolk noodles

Oil deep 19cm square cake pan; line base and sides with baking paper.

Combine cheese, yolks, 2 cloves of the garlic and 2 tablespoons of the chives in medium bowl; spread into prepared pan, smooth top. Cover pan with foil; place in baking dish with enough boiling water to come halfway up sides of pan. Bake in moderate oven about 1 hour or until firm; remove foil, bake about 10 minutes or until browned lightly. Remove from oven; remove pan from dish, allow to cool.

Boil wine in large pan until reduced by half. Add butter, remaining garlic and mushrooms; cook, stirring, until mushrooms are soft. Add remaining chives.

Meanwhile, cook noodles in large pan of boiling water, uncovered, until just tender; drain. Rinse under hot water; drain. Cover to keep warm.

Cut baked ricotta into 8 triangles; divide triangles among 4 serving plates. Place equal parts of noodles and mushroom mixture on triangles.

SERVES 4

Noodles and mushroom ragout best made just before serving. Baked ricotta can be made 1 day ahead

Storage Covered, in refrigerator

GOAT CHEESE AND ROAST VEGETABLE TERRINE

The sheet of fresh rice noodle used here, unfolded, looks like a big, white tea-towel. Use soon after buying them because the older they are, the more likely these noodles are to break; keep refrigerated.

1 large (500g) eggplant
2 medium (240g) yellow zucchini
4 medium (800g) red capsicums
250g English spinach, trimmed
200g mild firm goat cheese
1 egg, beaten
1 x 250g piece fresh rice noodle

LEMON MAYONNAISE
1 egg yolk
3 teaspoons Dijon mustard
1/2 teaspoon salt
2 teaspoons lemon juice
1/2 cup (125ml) light olive oil
1/2 teaspoon cracked black pepper
1/2 teaspoon grated lemon rind
2 tablespoons lemon juice, extra

Cut eggplant and zucchini lengthways into 5mm-wide slices. Place, in single layer, on oven trays; coat with cooking oil spray, grill until browned lightly.

Quarter capsicums; remove seeds and membranes. Roast under grill or in very hot oven, skin-side up, until skin blisters and blackens. Wrap capsicum pieces in plastic or paper for 5 minutes; peel.

Boil, steam or microwave spinach until tender; drain. Chop half the spinach roughly; combine with cheese and egg in large bowl.

Oil 15cm x 25cm loaf pan, line base with baking paper, extending paper over 2 long sides. Cut a 20cm x 40cm rectangle from noodle sheet; place in prepared pan, extending over 2 long sides. Top with the remaining spinach, half of the capsicum, cheese mixture, zucchini, remaining half of the capsicum, then the eggplant. Fold noodle sheets over eggplant; cover pan tightly with foil.

Bake in moderately slow oven 1 hour. Cool terrine 15 minutes before turning onto plate. Serve terrine, cut into slices, with Lemon Mayonnaise.

Lemon Mayonnaise Blend or process egg yolk, mustard, salt and juice until smooth. With motor operating, gradually pour in oil; process until thick. Stir in pepper, rind and extra juice.

SERVES 4 TO 6

Both terrine and mayonnaise can be prepared 1 day ahead

Storage Covered, separately, in refrigerator

ROAST WINTER VEGETABLES WITH SPLIT PEA SAUCE

We used a simple Chinese flat dried wheat noodle that was gutsy enough to be able to hold its own against the robust quality of the combined vegetables.

800g pumpkin, chopped
1 medium (225g) swede, chopped
2 medium (250g) parsnips, chopped
2 large (360g) carrots, chopped
1 large (200g) onion, sliced
6 cloves garlic, peeled
1/4 cup (60ml) olive oil
1 tablespoon sumac
300g dried wheat noodles
2 tablespoons chopped fresh
    coriander leaves

SPLIT PEA SAUCE

1/2 cup (100g) yellow split peas
3 cups (750ml) vegetable stock
1 small (80g) onion, chopped finely
2 cloves garlic, crushed
1 teaspoon ground cumin
1 teaspoon ground coriander
1 tablespoon lemon juice
1/4 cup (60ml) water

Brush vegetables with combined oil and sumac; place, in single layer, in large baking dish. Bake, uncovered, in hot oven about 30 minutes or until vegetables are browned and just tender.

Meanwhile, cook noodles in large pan of boiling water, uncovered, until just tender; drain. Cover to keep warm.

Combine vegetables in large bowl with noodles and coriander. Serve with hot Split Pea Sauce.

Split Pea Sauce Rinse peas under cold water; drain. Combine peas, 2 cups (500ml) of the stock, onion and garlic in a large pan. Bring to boil; simmer, uncovered, about 30 minutes or until peas are soft. Blend or process pea mixture with spices and combined remaining stock, juice and water until pureed. Return to pan; stir over heat until hot.

SERVES 6

Vegetables and noodles best prepared just before serving. Split pea sauce can be made 1 day ahead

Storage Covered, in refrigerator

Opposite Goat cheese and roast vegetable terrine
Below Roast winter vegetables with split pea sauce

DRIED EGG NOODLES are sometimes labelled tamago ramen, ba mee or dahn mein, and come in various thicknesses and colours from the addition of artificial or vegetable dyes. Some Asian dried egg noodles are very similar to their Italian cousins fettuccine and tagliatelle. In some recipes, fresh egg noodles can be used instead of dried if they are soaked (rather than boiled) in hot water just until tender. As in all noodle cases, feel free to use one for the other, bearing in mind the necessary differences in cooking times and methods.

BROAD BEAN, CHICKPEA AND LEMON THYME WITH NOODLES

The pulses make this dish seem Middle-Eastern in origin but the addition of lemon thyme and aged parmesan makes it a unique dish that succeeds on its own merits.

$2/3$ cup (130g) **dried chickpeas**

$1/3$ cup (80ml) **olive oil**

1 large (200g) **onion, chopped**

3 medium (600g) **red capsicums, seeded, chopped**

2 cloves **garlic, crushed**

3 medium (570g) **tomatoes, peeled, seeded, chopped**

1 cup (250ml) **vegetable stock**

1 teaspoon **sugar**

500g **frozen broad beans, cooked, peeled**

$1^1/2$ tablespoons **chopped fresh lemon thyme leaves**

$1/3$ cup (25g) **finely grated parmesan cheese**

250g **dried egg noodles**

$1/2$ cup (40g) **parmesan cheese flakes**

Cover chickpeas with cold water in medium bowl; stand, covered, overnight.

Drain chickpeas then cook, uncovered, in medium pan of boiling water until just tender; drain.

Meanwhile, heat oil in large pan; cook onion, capsicum and garlic, stirring, 15 minutes. Add tomato; cook, stirring, 10 minutes. Add stock, sugar and chickpeas; cook, covered, 5 minutes. Add broad beans, thyme and grated cheese; stir until just heated through.

Meanwhile, cook noodles in large pan of boiling water, uncovered, until just tender; drain. Gently toss noodles in large bowl with bean mixture; top with cheese.

SERVES 4

Best made just before serving

Above Broad bean, chickpea and lemon thyme with noodles
Right Beetroot-tinted noodles with white beans

BEETROOT-TINTED NOODLES WITH WHITE BEANS

Similar in appearance to a fine tagliolini, the dried Chinese flat wheat noodle used in this recipe was porous enough to absorb the beetroot colour extremely well.

1 cup (200g) dried cannellini beans
2 medium (320g) raw
beetroot, grated
350g dried wheat noodles
2 tablespoons vegetable oil
5 cloves garlic, crushed
2 tablespoons coarsely grated
lemon rind
12 fresh water chestnuts, chopped

1/2 cup (125ml) olive oil
1/4 cup (60ml) balsamic vinegar
1/4 cup (60ml) lemon juice
2 tablespoons chopped fresh chives
2 teaspoons sugar

Cover beans with cold water in medium bowl; stand, covered, overnight.

Drain beans then cook, uncovered, in medium pan of boiling water until just tender; drain.

Bring 1.5 litres (6 cups) water to boil in large pan; simmer beetroot, uncovered, 5 minutes. Add noodles to pan; return to boil then remove from heat immediately. Stand, stirring occasionally, until noodles are just tender and have absorbed beetroot colour. Drain; cover to keep warm.

Heat oil in wok or large pan; stir-fry beans, garlic, rind and water chestnuts, until water chestnuts are just tender and browned lightly. Stir in combined remaining ingredients; cook, stirring, until heated through. Divide noodles among serving plates; top with water chestnut mixture.

SERVES 4 TO 6

Best made just before serving

MEXI-VEGIES WITH TOASTED TORTILLA CHIPS

This "South of the Border" combination of ingredients makes a wonderfully satisfying main course for a Saturday night supper.

1 tablespoon olive oil
1 medium (150g) onion, sliced
2 teaspoons ground cumin
2 teaspoons ground coriander
3 small (750g) kumara, chopped
**1 medium (200g) red
   capsicum, chopped**
**1 medium (200g) yellow
   capsicum, chopped**
2 (800g) corn cobs, chopped
**425g can Mexe-Beans (pinto beans
   in chilli sauce)**
400g can tomatoes
1 cup (250ml) vegetable stock
6 x 25cm packaged flour tortillas
125g dried rice noodles
**1 cup (125g) coarsely grated
   cheddar cheese**

AVOCADO CREAM
2 small (550g) avocados
1/3 cup (80ml) sour cream
1 tablespoon lemon juice
**1 medium (190) tomato, peeled,
   seeded, chopped**
**1 small (100g) red onion,
   chopped finely**
**2 tablespoons chopped fresh
   coriander leaves**

Heat oil in large pan; cook onion, stirring, until soft. Add cumin and coriander; cook, stirring, 1 minute. Stir in kumara, capsicums, corn, beans, undrained crushed tomatoes and stock. Bring to boil; simmer, uncovered, about 15 minutes or until corn is tender.

Cut each tortilla into 6 wedge-shaped pieces, place on oven tray in single layer; toast in moderate oven about 5 minutes or until crisp and browned lightly.

Meanwhile, place noodles in large heatproof bowl, cover with boiling water, stand until just tender; drain. Rinse under cold water; drain.

Gently stir noodles into vegetable mixture; divide mixture among 6 flameproof serving dishes. Sprinkle with cheese; grill until cheese melts.

Serve Mexi-Vegies accompanied with tortilla chips and Avocado Cream.

Avocado Cream Blend or process avocados, sour cream and juice until just smooth; place in medium serving bowl, stir in tomato, onion and coriander.

SERVES 6

Best made just before serving

Above Mexi-vegies with toasted tortilla chips
Opposite Creamy spinach and ricotta pancake torte

CREAMY SPINACH AND RICOTTA PANCAKE TORTE

Fresh egg noodles form part of the batter for this luscious stack of pancakes sandwiched with a creamy cheese, toasted pine nut and fresh spinach filling.

1kg English spinach, trimmed
600g ricotta cheese
1/3 cup (50g) pine nuts, toasted
2 tablespoons cream
200g fresh egg noodles
3/4 cup (75g) plain flour
3 eggs, beaten
1 cup (250ml) milk

TOMATO AND CAPSICUM SAUCE

2 medium (400g) red capsicums
2 cloves garlic, unpeeled
1/4 cup (60ml) olive oil
1 large (200g) onion, chopped
2 x 400g cans tomatoes
1/4 cup firmly packed chopped fresh basil leaves

Boil, steam or microwave spinach until just wilted; drain. Rinse under cold water; drain. Squeeze as much liquid as possible from spinach; chop finely. Combine spinach with cheese, nuts and cream in large bowl.

Cook noodles in large pan of boiling water, uncovered, until just tender; drain. Rinse under cold water; drain. Chop noodles coarsely.

Sift flour into large bowl; gradually stir in combined eggs and milk, beat until smooth. Stir in noodles. Pour a quarter of the noodle mixture into large heated oiled pan, spread to 20cm circle; cook until browned lightly both sides. Repeat with remaining mixture.

Place 1 pancake into deep 20cm-round cake pan, spread over a third of the spinach mixture; top with another pancake. Repeat layering with remaining pancakes and spinach mixture, finishing with a pancake.

Bake, covered, in moderate oven about 30 minutes or until heated through. Cut into wedges, serve with warmed Tomato and Capsicum Sauce.

Tomato and Capsicum Sauce Quarter capsicums; remove and discard seeds and membranes. Roast capsicum and garlic with 2 tablespoons of the oil in small baking dish, uncovered, in moderately hot oven 30 minutes. Remove from pan. Cover capsicum with plastic or paper; stand 5 minutes, peel away skin. Squeeze pulp from unpeeled garlic into small bowl.

Meanwhile, heat remaining oil in pan; cook onion, stirring, until soft. Add undrained crushed tomatoes, bring to boil; simmer, uncovered, 5 minutes. Blend or process tomato mixture with capsicum, garlic pulp and basil until almost smooth.

SERVES 6

Best made just before serving. Tomato and capsicum sauce can be made 1 day ahead

Storage Covered, in refrigerator

NOODLE PRIMAVERA

Our variation of the Italian classic sauce is so good you'll want to use it all the time — regardless of whether or not you use the fresh egg noodles shown here or the more traditional dried fettuccine.

1 tablespoon olive oil
1 medium (150g) onion, sliced
1 clove garlic, crushed
500g asparagus, trimmed, cut into
**   4cm pieces**
2 cups (250g) frozen peas
400ml creme fraiche
¹/₄ cup (60ml) vegetable stock
2 tablespoons Dijon mustard
¹/₃ cup (25g) coarsely grated
**   parmesan cheese**
¹/₄ cup chopped fresh mint leaves
375g fresh egg noodles

Heat oil in large pan; cook onion and garlic, stirring, until onion is soft. Add asparagus; cook, stirring, about 1 minute or until almost tender. Add peas and combined creme fraiche, stock and mustard; cook, over medium heat, stirring, about 5 minutes or until thickened slightly. Stir in cheese and mint.

Meanwhile, cook noodles in large pan of boiling water, uncovered, until just tender; drain. Gently toss noodles in large bowl with asparagus mixture.

SERVES 4 TO 6

Best made just before serving

Above Noodle primavera
Above right Eggplant, tomato and bocconcini towers
Right Tofu and vegetable curry

Add blended milk powder and water, b [ ] leaves, cinnamon stick and pumpkin. Bring to boil; simmer, covered, until pumpkin is almost tender. Add beans and capsicum; simmer until beans are just tender. Add tofu; stir until just heated through.

Meanwhile, cook noodles in large pan of boiling water, uncovered, until just tender; drain. Divide noodles among serving bowls; top with vegetable curry.

SERVES 6

Best made just before serving

EGGPLANT, TOMATO AND BOCCONCINI TOWERS

Substitute rice vermicelli if you prefer for the bean thread noodles we used.

60g bean thread noodles
1/3 cup (80ml) vegetable oil
2 small (460g) eggplants
3 medium (225g) egg tomatoes, sliced
1/4 cup (60ml) balsamic vinegar
1/4 cup (60ml) olive oil
90g bocconcini cheese

PESTO
1 cup firmly packed fresh basil leaves
1/2 cup (40g) coarsely grated parmesan cheese
2 cloves garlic
1 tablespoon olive oil
1 tablespoon pine nuts, toasted
1/4 cup (60ml) buttermilk

Place noodles in medium heatproof bowl, cover with boiling water, stand until just tender; drain. Pat dry with absorbent paper. Heat vegetable oil in small pan; shallow-fry 20g bundles of noodles, in batches, until just browned. Drain bundles on absorbent paper; you need 12 bundles.

Cut each eggplant into 6 slices; place on wire rack. Sprinkle eggplant slices with salt; stand 30 minutes. Rinse eggplant thoroughly under cold water; pat dry with absorbent paper.

Place eggplant and tomato slices on oiled oven tray; brush with combined vinegar and olive oil. Grill eggplant, both sides, until browned lightly.

Cut cheese into 5mm slices. Top 6 of the noodle bundles with a slice of eggplant, tomato, cheese and some of the Pesto. Repeat layering, ending with cheese and a drizzle of Pesto.

Pesto Blend or process all ingredients until pureed.

SERVES 6

Pesto can be made 1 day ahead

Storage Covered, in refrigerator

TOFU AND VEGETABLE CURRY

We used fresh egg noodles but use whatever you like since the noodle here merely replaces the rice usually eaten with a curry.

2 tablespoons peanut oil
2 large (400g) onions, sliced
1/4 cup (40g) curry powder
1 1/2 cups (200g) coconut milk powder
3 cups (750ml) boiling water
4 bay leaves
1 cinnamon stick
600g butternut pumpkin, peeled, cut into 2.5cm pieces
100g green beans, trimmed, halved
1 medium (200g) red capsicum, chopped
200g firm fresh tofu, drained, chopped
200g fresh egg noodles

Heat oil in large pan; cook onions, stirring, until soft. Add curry powder; cook, stirring, about 1 minute or until fragrant.

QUARTET OF BEANS IN A CHILLI LIME SAUCE

Arrowroot noodles are notable more for their interesting texture than their flavour. Substitute bean thread noodles if you wish.

270g arrowroot noodles
250g frozen broad beans,
  thawed, peeled
150g green beans, sliced
150g snake beans, sliced
150g butter beans, sliced
vegetable oil, for deep-frying
1/4 cup (40g) capers, drained
1 tablespoon olive oil
6 cloves garlic, crushed
1 small (100g) red onion, chopped
4 small fresh red chillies, seeded
2 tablespoons finely grated lime rind
1/2 cup (125ml) vegetable stock
2/3 cup (160ml) cream
12 (60g) black olives,
  seeded, sliced

Cook noodles in large pan of boiling water, uncovered, until just tender; drain. Rinse under cold water; drain.

Boil, steam or microwave beans, separately, until just tender; drain. Heat vegetable oil in small pan; deep-fry capers until crisp. Drain on absorbent paper.

Heat olive oil in wok or large pan; stir-fry garlic, onion, chilli and rind until onion is soft. Add stock, cream, olives, beans and noodles; cook, stirring gently, until sauce thickens and mixture is heated through.

SERVES 4

Best made just before serving

Below Quartet of beans in a chilli lime sauce
Opposite Tempura on rice-sticks with beetroot chips

TEMPURA ON RICE-STICKS WITH BEETROOT CHIPS

Any noodle can be used here, but deep-fried rice sticks harmonise nicely with the crunch of the tempura and beetroot.

vegetable oil, for deep-frying
120g dried rice noodles
2 large (400g) raw beetroot
2 egg yolks
2 cups (500ml) iced water
1 1/3 cups (200g) plain flour
150g firm tofu, cubed
100g snow peas, trimmed
1 bunch (250g) asparagus,
  trimmed, sliced
1 large (150g) green
  zucchini, sliced
2 medium (240g) yellow
  zucchini, sliced
100g green beans, sliced
1 large (200g) red onion, sliced
2 cups (200g) chopped cauliflower
rice flour
1/4 cup (60ml) mirin
1/2 cup (60ml) light soy sauce
1 tablespoon sugar
1 tablespoon sweet chilli sauce

Heat vegetable oil in large pan; deep-fry noodles, in batches, until puffed. Drain noodles on absorbent paper.

Using a vegetable peeler, slice beetroot into paper-thin strips. Reheat same oil; deep-fry beetroot, in batches, until crisp. Drain on absorbent paper.

Just before serving, combine egg yolks and water in medium bowl; stir in sifted flour all at once. Do not overmix; mixture should be lumpy.

Reheat vegetable oil in same pan. Toss tofu and all vegetables in rice flour; shake off excess. Dip tofu and vegetables, 1 at a time, in batter. Deep-fry tofu and vegetables until browned lightly; drain on absorbent paper. Divide noodles among serving plates; top with tempura tofu and vegetables. Serve with sauce made with combined remaining ingredients and crisp beetroot chips.

SERVES 4

Best made just before serving

▭ **ARROWROOT NOODLES** are semi-transparent, off-white noodles made, not surprisingly, from starch extracted from arrowroot tubers. They are a favoured ingredient in the spicy cuisine of the western Chinese province of Sichuan, and in Korea, a cold-climate country where these noodles feature in hearty soups.

ROASTED TOMATOES WITH SAUCY BASIL NOODLES

Fresh egg noodles are the perfect foil for this rich sauce and luscious tomatoes.

12 medium (900g) egg tomatoes
1 teaspoon salt
1 teaspoon freshly cracked black pepper
1 teaspoon sugar
2 cups firmly packed fresh basil leaves
1 clove garlic, peeled
1/4 cup (20g) coarsely grated parmesan cheese
1/3 cup (80ml) olive oil
1 tablespoon balsamic vinegar
80g prosciutto, sliced finely
375g fresh egg noodles
1/3 cup (50g) pine nuts, toasted

Halve tomatoes; place, cut-side up, on wire rack in baking dish. Sprinkle with combined salt, pepper and sugar; bake in moderately hot oven about 30 minutes or until soft.

Blend or process basil, garlic, cheese, oil and vinegar until almost pureed.

Place prosciutto, in single layer, on oven tray; grill until crisp, turning once during cooking.

Meanwhile, cook noodles in large pan of boiling water, uncovered, until just tender; drain.

Gently toss basil mixture in large bowl with noodles; divide among serving plates. Top with tomato halves and prosciutto; sprinkle with pine nuts.

SERVES 4 TO 6

Best made just before serving

GLOSSARY

BACON RASHERS also known as slices of bacon; made of cured and smoked pork side.

BANANA LEAVES can be ordered from fruit and vegetable stores. Usually 1 leaf is cut into about 10 pieces. Cut with a sharp knife close to the main stem then immerse in hot water so that leaves will be pliable.

BEAN CURD see **Tofu**.

BEETROOT also known as beets.

BLACK BEANS are salted, fermented and dried soy beans. Soak, drain and rinse dried beans; chop before, or mash during, cooking to release flavour. **Black bean sauce** is made from fermented

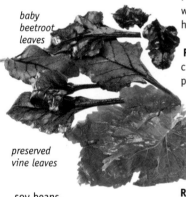

baby beetroot leaves

preserved vine leaves

soy beans, spices, water and wheat flour.

BLINI also known as blintzes. Buckwheat pancakes originally from Russia where they were eaten with caviar. Their fillings can be sweet for desserts, or savoury for finger foods.

BONITO FLAKES a dried fish from the mackerel family, available both in flaked form and as an ingredient in the Japanese stock, dashi.

BREADCRUMBS stale 1- or 2-day-old bread made into crumbs by grating, blending or processing.

BUTTERMILK low-fat milk cultured to give it a slightly sour, tangy taste; low-fat yogurt can be substituted.

CHEESE

Bocconcini small rounds of fresh "baby" mozzarella, traditionally made in Italy from buffalo milk. Spoils rapidly so must be refrigerated, in brine, for a maximum of 2 days.
Cheddar use an aged, hard, strong-flavoured variety.
Fetta Greek in origin; a crumbly goat or sheep milk cheese having a pronounced sharp, salty taste.
Goat made from goat milk, has an earthy, strong taste; comes in both soft and firm textures.
Haloumi a firm, cream-coloured sheep milk cheese matured in brine; somewhat like a minty, salty fetta in flavour. Good grilled.
Mozzarella a semi-soft cheese with a delicate, fresh taste; has a low melting point and stringy texture when heated.
Pecorino hard, dry, yellow cheese, which has a sharp, pungent taste. Originally from sheep milk, now made with cow milk. If unavailable, use parmesan.
Ricotta a sweet, fairly moist, fresh-curd cheese with a fairly low-fat content.
Romano a hard, straw-coloured cheese with a grainy texture and sharp, tangy flavour; usually made from a combination of cow and goat or sheep milk. A good cheese for grating.
Smoked cheddar a hard cheddar cheese which has been placed, un-cut, in a smoke room for about 6 hours. There is also artificially smoked cheese where flavour is added to the milk before the cheese is made.

CHERMOULLA spicy Moroccan mixture of fresh and ground spices including coriander, cumin and paprika. This paste may be covered with a thin layer of oil to preserve it.

CHICKPEAS also called garbanzos; an irregularly round, sandy-coloured legume used extensively in Mediterranean, Asian and Hispanic cooking.

CHILLI SAUCE
Hot we used a hot Chinese variety made from bird's-eye chillies, salt and vinegar. Use sparingly, increasing the quantity to your taste.
Sweet a comparatively mild, Thai-type commercial sauce made from red chillies, sugar, garlic and vinegar.

CHINESE BARBECUED PORK
also known as char siew. Traditionally cooked in special ovens, this pork has a sweet-sticky coating made from soy sauce, sherry, five-spice and hoisin sauce. It is available from Asian food stores.

COCONUT
Cream available in cans and cartons; made from coconut and water.
Milk pure, unsweetened coconut milk available in cans.
Milk powder coconut milk that has been dehydrated and ground to a fine powder.

CORN KERNELS also known as niblets.

black mussels

chorizo sausage

black olives

kalamata olives

CORNFLOUR also known as cornstarch.

CREAM
Fresh (minimum fat content 35%) also known as pure cream and pouring cream; has no additives like commercially thickened cream.
Sour (minimum fat content 35%) a thick, commercially cultured soured cream.

CREME FRAICHE a fresh matured cream that has been commercially lightly soured (minimum fat content 35%); available in cartons from delicatessens and supermarkets. To make creme fraiche, combine 300ml cream with 300ml sour cream in bowl; cover, stand at room temperature until mixture thickens. This will take 1 or 2 days, depending on room temperature; refrigerate once fermented. This makes about 2$\frac{1}{2}$ cups (625ml).

CURRY
Madras paste consists of coriander, cumin, pepper, turmeric, chilli, garlic, ginger, vinegar and oil.
Powder a blend of ground spices used for convenience when making

clams

large white scallops

ground turmeric

fresh turmeric

sumac

sweet Spanish paprika

hot paprika

baby capers

regular capers

ground cumin

cumin seeds

Indian food. Can consist of some of the following spices in varying proportions: dried chilli, cinnamon, coriander, cumin, fennel, fenugreek, mace, cardamom and turmeric. Choose mild or hot to suit your taste and the recipe.

Red paste consisting of chilli, onion, garlic, oil, lemon rind, shrimp paste, cumin, paprika, turmeric and pepper.

DASHI the basic fish and seaweed stock that accounts for the distinctive flavour of many Japanese dishes. It is made from dried bonito flakes and kelp (kombu). Instant dashi powder, also known as dashi-no-moto, is a concentrated granulated powder. Available from Asian speciality stores.

EGGS some recipes in this book call for raw or barely cooked eggs; exercise caution if there is a salmonella problem in your area.

FISH AND SHELLFISH
Atlantic salmon originally from Atlantic coastal waters, now farmed all over the world. Available whole, or as steaks, cutlets or fillets.
Barramundi large fish found in coastal rivers of northern Australia and the Pacific. It has a firm, white flesh with a large flake and mild flavour. Available whole, as steaks, cutlets or fillets. If unavailable, use perch.
Crab meat sweet, succulent flesh from fresh crabs. Use canned if fresh is unavailable.
Ling an excellent eating fish with white, firm flesh. When cooked, it is moist with a large flake. Usually available as skinless fillets.

FISH SAUCE also called nam pla or nuoc nam; made from pulverised, salted, fermented fish, most often anchovies. Has a pungent smell and strong taste. There are many different fish sauces on the market, and the intensity of flavour varies with each one.

FLOUR
Plain an all-purpose flour, made from wheat.
Rice a very fine flour, made from ground white rice.

GARAM MASALA a blend of spices, originating in North India; based on varying proportions of cardamom, cinnamon, cloves, coriander, fennel and cumin, roasted and ground together. Black pepper and chilli can be added, to make a hotter example.

GHERKIN sometimes known as a cornichon; young, dark-green cucumbers grown especially for pickling.

HOISIN SAUCE a thick, sweet and spicy Chinese paste made from salted fermented soy beans, onions and garlic; used as a marinade or baste, or to accent stir-fries and barbecued or roasted foods.

KETJAP MANIS Indonesian sweet, thick soy sauce which has sugar and spices added.

MINCED MEAT also known as ground meat, as in beef, pork, lamb and veal.

MISO is grouped into 2 main categories — red and white, although the "red" is dark brown in colour and "white" is more the colour of weak tea. Made in Japan, miso is a paste made from cooked, mashed, salted and fermented soy beans, and it is a common ingredient in soups, sauces and dressings. Also known as misi.

MORTAR AND PESTLE used for grinding, the mortar being the bowl and the pestle the grinding implement. Used for spices and pastes.

MUSLIN plain, finely woven cotton fabric. Often used to strain stocks and sauces. If unavailable, use disposable coffee filter papers.

MUSTARD
Dijon a distinctively sharp French mustard.
Seeded a coarse-grain; made of crushed mustard seeds and Dijon-style mustard.

NORI a type of dried seaweed used in Japanese cooking as a flavouring, garnish or for sushi. Sold in thin sheets.

OIL
Hazelnut a mono-unsaturated oil, made in France, extracted from crushed hazelnuts.
Olive a mono-unsaturated oil, made from the pressing of tree-ripened olives; especially good for everyday cooking and in salad dressings. Light describes the mild flavour, not the fat level.

baby bok choy

rocket

canned green peppercorns

Sichuan peppercorns

black peppercorns

star anise

Chinese cabbage

English spinach

choy sum

baby English spinach leaves

Peanut pressed from ground peanuts; most commonly used oil in Asian cooking because of its high smoke point.
Sesame made from roasted, crushed, white sesame seeds; a flavouring rather than a cooking medium.
Vegetable any of a number of oils sourced from plants rather than animal fats.

OYSTER SAUCE Asian in origin, rich, brown sauce made from oysters, brine, salt and soy sauce then thickened.

PITTA also known as pita, Lebanese bread or pocket bread; a Middle Eastern, wheat-flour bread, usually sold pre-packaged in large, flat pieces easily separated into two paper-thin rounds. Comes in smaller, thicker pieces commonly called **Pocket Pitta.**

PLUM SAUCE a thick, sweet and sour dipping sauce made from plums, vinegar, sugar, chillies and spices.

PROSCIUTTO salted-cured, air-dried (unsmoked), pressed ham or lamb; usually sold in paper-thin slices, ready to eat.

PUFF PASTRY SHEETS frozen sheets of puff pastry (measuring 24.5cm square) made from wheat flour; vegetable margarine or butter, salt, food acid and water.

RICE
Calrose is a medium grain rice that is extremely versatile; can substitute for short- or long-grain rice if necessary.

RICE PAPER mostly from Vietnam (banh trang). Made from rice paste and stamped into rounds with a woven pattern. Stores well at room temperature, although

coriander roots

fresh and dried kaffir lime leaves

dried bay leaves

they are quite brittle and will break if dropped. Dipped momentarily in water they become pliable wrappers for fried food and for eating fresh (uncooked) vegetables.

SAMBAL OELEK (also ulek or olek) Indonesian in origin; a salty paste made from ground chillies.

SCORE shallow cuts in a criss-cross pattern, over meat vegetables or seafood. Often used on squid.

SEASONED PEPPER a packaged preparation of combined black pepper, red capsicum (bell pepper) and p

SHERRY fortified wine consumed as an aperitif or used in cooking. Sold as fino (light, dry), amontillado (medium sweet, dark) and oloroso (full-bodied, very dark).

SHRIMP PASTE also known as trasi or blanchan; it is a strong-scented, almost solid, preserved paste made of salted dried shrimp. Used as a pungent flavouring in many Southeast Asian soups and sauces.

SOY SAUCE made from fermented soy beans. Several variations are available in most supermarkets and Asian food stores.
Dark used for colour as well as flavour, particularly in North Chinese cooking.
Light as the name suggests, is light in colour. We used a light soy sauce of Japanese origin. It is light in colour but generally quite salty.
Salt-reduced a soy sauce with 46% of the salt removed.

SPATCHCOCK a small chicken (poussin), no more than 6 weeks old, weighing a maximum 500g.

SPRING ROLL WRAPPERS are also sometimes called egg roll wrappers; they come in various

sizes and can be purchased fresh or frozen from Asian supermarkets. Made from a delicate wheat-based pastry, they can be used for making gow gee and samosas as well as spring rolls.

SUGAR we used coarse, granulated table sugar, also known as crystal sugar, unless otherwise specified.
Brown a soft, fine, granulated sugar containing molasses to give its characteristic colour.
Palm very fine sugar from the coconut palm. It is sold in cakes, also known as gula jawa, gula melaka and jaggery. Palm sugar can be substituted with brown or black sugar.
Raw a naturally golden brown, granulated sugar.

SULTANAS golden raisins.

SUMAC a purple-red, astringent spice ground from berries growing on shrubs that flourish wild around the Mediterranean and even further east to Iran, where it is sprinkled over the national dish of grilled meat and steamed rice. Good in salad dressings and sauces.

TAMARIND CONCENTRATE a thick, purple-black, ready-to-use paste extracted from the pulp of the tamarind bean; used as is, with no soaking, stirred into sauces, dressings and casseroles.

button

shiitake

shimeji

Swiss brown

enoki

oyster

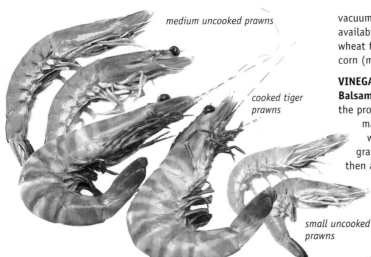

medium uncooked prawns

cooked tiger prawns

small uncooked prawns

vacuum-packed. Two kinds are available, one made from wheat flour and the other from corn (maizemeal).

VINEGAR
Balsamic authentic only from the province of Modena, Italy; made from a regional wine of white Trebbiano grapes specially processed then aged in antique wooden casks to give it its uniquely exquisite, pungent flavour.

with sugar and salt. Also sometimes called seasoned rice vinegar.
White made from spirit of cane sugar.
White wine made from fermented white wine.

WASABI an Asian horseradish used to make a fiery sauce traditionally served with Japanese raw fish dishes.

WATER CHESTNUTS resemble chestnuts in appearance, hence the English name. They

TERIYAKI SAUCE a homemade or commercially bottled sauce usually made from soy sauce, mirin, sugar, ginger and other spices; it imparts a distinctive glaze when brushed on grilled meat.

TOFU also known as bean curd, an off-white, custard-like product made from the "milk" of crushed soy beans; comes fresh as soft or firm, and processed as fried or pressed dried sheets. Leftover fresh tofu can be refrigerated, in water (which is changed daily), for up to 4 days. Silken tofu refers to the method it's made by, strained through silk, rather than its texture.
Bean curd pouches pockets of fried bean curd (tofu) which are

able to be opened out to take a filling. Available from Asian food stores.

TOMATO
Paste a concentrated tomato puree used to flavour and thicken soups, stews, sauces and casseroles.
Puree canned pureed tomatoes (not tomato paste). Substitute with fresh peeled and pureed tomatoes.
Sun-dried (dehydrated tomatoes) we use sun-dried tomatoes packaged in oil, unless otherwise specified.

TORTILLA thin, round, unleavened bread originating in Mexico; can be made at home or purchased frozen, fresh or

plain nori

toasted nori

fresh water chestnuts

bean curd pouches

canned water chestnuts

Cider made from fermented apples.
Raspberry made from fresh raspberries steeped in a white wine vinegar.
Red wine based on fermented red wine.
Rice made from fermented rice, colourless and flavoured

are small brown tubers with a crisp, white, nutty-tasting flesh. Their crunchy texture is best experienced fresh, however, canned water chestnuts are more easily obtained and can be kept about a month, once opened, under refrigeration.

WONTON WRAPPERS fresh pastry sheets made with egg; substitute spring roll wrappers.

WORCESTERSHIRE SAUCE a thin, dark-brown spicy sauce used as a seasoning for meat, gravies and cocktails and as a condiment.

sesame seeds

polenta

black mustard seeds

red lentils

yellow split peas

INDEX

FACTS AND FIGURES

Wherever you live in the world, you can use our recipes with the help of our easy-to-follow conversions for all your cooking needs. These conversions are approximate only. The difference between the exact and approximate conversion of liquid and dry measures amounts to only a teaspoon or two, and will not make any difference to your cooking results.

Measuring Equipment

The difference between measuring cups internationally is minimal within 2 or 3 teaspoons' difference. The most accurate way of measuring dry ingredients is to weigh them. When measuring liquids, use a clear glass or plastic jug with the metric markings.

In this book, we use metric measuring cups and spoons approved by Standards Australia:

- *1 cup: 250ml*
- *1 teaspoon: 5ml*
- *1 tablespoon: 20ml*

How to Measure

When using metric measuring cups, it is important to shake the dry ingredients loosely into the required cup. Do not tap the cup, or pack ingredients into the cup unless otherwise directed. Level the top of the cup with a knife.

When using metric measuring spoons, level the top of the spoon with a knife. When measuring liquids in the jug, place the jug on a flat surface, and check for accuracy at eye level.

We use large eggs with an average weight of 60g.

DRY MEASURES

Metric	Imperial
15g	½oz
60g	2oz
90g	3oz
125g	4oz (¼lb)
250g	8oz (½lb)
280g	9oz
315g	10oz
345g	11oz
375g	12oz (¾lb)
410g	13oz
440g	14oz
470g	15oz
500g	16oz (1lb)
750g	24oz (1½lb)
1kg	32oz (2lb)

Note: NZ, Canada, USA and UK all use 15ml tablespoons. All cup and spoon measurements are level.

HELPFUL MEASURES

Metric	Imperial
3mm	⅛in
6mm	¼in
2.5cm	1in
8cm	3in
10cm	4in
15cm	6in
20cm	8in
28cm	11in
30cm	12in (1ft)

LIQUID MEASURES

Metric	Imperial
30ml	1 fluid oz
125ml	4 fluid oz
150ml	5 fluid oz (¼ pint/1 gill)
250ml	8 fluid oz
300ml	10 fluid oz (½ pint)
1000ml (1 litre)	1¾ pints

OVEN TEMPERATURES

These oven temperatures are only a guide. Always check the manufacturer's manual.

	C° (Celsius)	F° (Fahrenheit)	Gas Mark
Very slow	120	250	1
Slow	150	300	2
Moderately slow	160	325	3
Moderate	180 - 190	350 - 375	4
Moderately hot	200 - 210	400 - 425	5
Hot	220 - 230	450 - 475	6
Very hot	240 - 250	500 - 525	7

Make Your Own Stock

Recipes can be made 4 days ahead: store, covered, in refrigerator; or freeze in smaller quantities. Remove any fat from the surface after stock has been refrigerated overnight.

Stock is available in cans or tetra packs. If using stock cubes or powder, use 1 teaspoon of stock powder or 1 small cube with 1 cup (250ml) water to give a strong stock. Check salt and fat content of packaged stocks. Recipes make 2.5 litres (10 cups).

CHICKEN STOCK

2kg chicken bones
2 medium (300g) onions, chopped
2 celery sticks, chopped
2 medium (250g) carrots, chopped
3 bay leaves
2 teaspoons black peppercorns
5 litres (20 cups) water

Combine all ingredients in large pan, simmer, uncovered, 2 hours; strain.

VEGETABLE STOCK

2 large (360g) carrots, chopped
2 large (360g) parsnips, chopped
4 medium (600g) onions, chopped
12 celery sticks, chopped
4 bay leaves
2 teaspoons black peppercorns
6 litres (24 cups) water

Combine all ingredients in large pan, simmer, uncovered, 1½ hours; strain.

BEEF STOCK

2kg meaty beef bones
2 medium (300g) onions
2 celery sticks, chopped
2 medium (250g) carrots, chopped
3 bay leaves
2 teaspoons black peppercorns
5 litres (20 cups) water
3 litres (12 cups) water, extra

Place bones and unpeeled chopped onions in baking dish. Bake in hot oven about 1 hour or until bones and onions are well browned. Transfer bones and onions to large pan, add celery, carrots, bay leaves, peppercorns and water, simmer, uncovered, 3 hours. Add extra water, simmer, uncovered, further 1 hour; strain.

Life's easier with these great Home Library gifts

Protect your favourite cookbooks and keep them clean, tidy and within easy reach with this smart vinyl folder. PLUS you can follow our recipes perfectly with a set of measuring cups and spoons, as used in the Women's Weekly Test Kitchen.

TO ORDER YOUR BOOK HOLDER OR MEASURING SET:

Price: Book Holder $11.95 (Australia); elsewhere $A21.95.
Metric Measuring Set $5.95 (Australia); $A8.00 (New Zealand); $A9.95 elsewhere
prices include postage and handling. This offer is available in all countries.

Phone: Have your credit card details ready. Sydney: (02) 9260 0035; **elsewhere in Australia:** 1800 252 515 (free call, Mon-Fri, 8.30am-5.30pm) or FAX your order to (02) 9267 4363 or MAIL your order by photocopying or completing the coupon below.

Payment: **Australian residents:** we accept the credit cards listed, money orders and cheques. **Overseas residents:** we accept the credit cards listed, drafts in $A drawn on an Australian bank, and also English, New Zealand and U.S. cheques in the currency of the country of issue. Credit card charges are at the exchange rate current at the time of payment.

Complete coupon and fax or post to:
AWW Home Library Reader Offer, ACP Direct, PO Box 7036, Sydney NSW 1028.